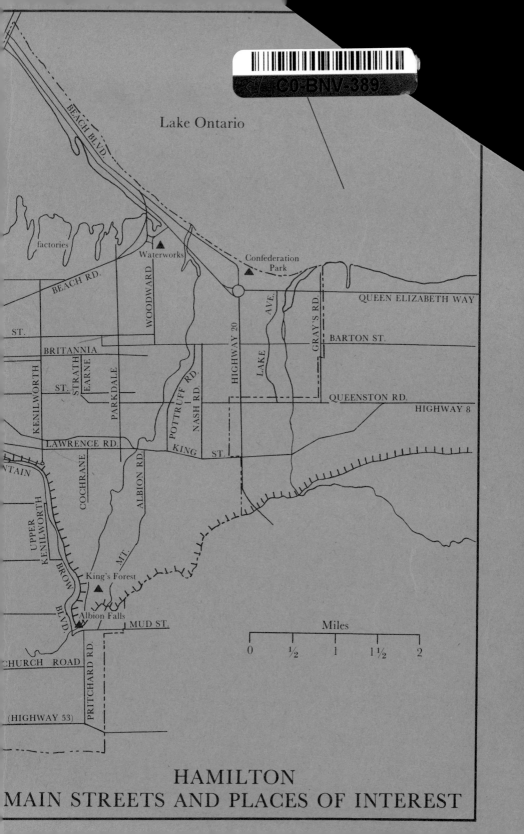

Lake Ontario

factories

BEACH BLVD.

Waterworks

Confederation Park

BEACH RD.

WOODWARD

QUEEN ELIZABETH WAY

ST.

HIGHWAY 20

LAKE AVE.

GRAY'S RD.

BARTON ST.

BRITANNIA

KENILWORTH

STRATH EARNE

ST.

PARKDALE

POTTRUFF RD.

NASH RD.

QUEENSTON RD.

HIGHWAY 8

LAWRENCE RD.

COCHRANE

ALBION RD.

KING   ST.

NTAIN

UPPER KENILWORTH

BROW

MT.

King's Forest

BLVD.

Albion Falls

MUD ST.

Miles

0   ½   1   1½   2

CHURCH ROAD

PRITCHARD RD.

(HIGHWAY 53)

HAMILTON
MAIN STREETS AND PLACES OF INTEREST

HAMILTON

The Story of a City

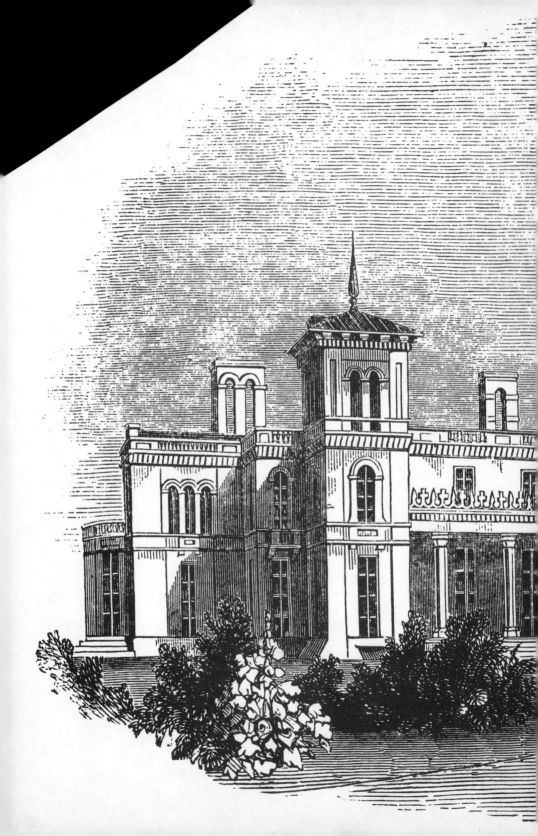

LOIS C. EVANS

HAMILTON

The Story of a City

ILLUSTRATIONS BY PUPILS
OF THE BURKHOLDER SCHOOL
HAMILTON, ONTARIO

PUBLISHED BY ORDER OF
THE BOARD OF EDUCATION
FOR THE CITY OF HAMILTON

THE RYERSON PRESS
TORONTO WINNIPEG VANCOUVER

PRINTED AND BOUND IN CANADA BY
THE RYERSON PRESS TORONTO

Foreword

As a centennial project, the Board of Education for the City of Hamilton commissioned Miss Lois C. Evans, B.A., M.Ed., to write an historical textbook on the history of Hamilton for the use of Senior Elementary School students.

This volume is the result of that commission. It can be used to supplement the course of study in Canadian History as laid down by the Department of Education.

The historical sketches were done by a group of students from Burkholder Elementary School.

GORDON E. PRICE,
Director of Education.

Preface

To tell Hamilton's story in a volume of this size is a difficult task. Scores of incidents, hundreds of anecdotes and thousands of individuals have been omitted. However, if this skeletal outline of Hamilton's growth and development should stimulate in even one student a continuing interest in his city's bygones, it will have served a communal purpose. It is hoped that the somewhat lengthy bibliography will be of some use to those readers who wish to pursue the study of a particular topic.

I should like to pay tribute to the two gentlemen who were responsible for my own love of local history. In the fall of 1948 when I was a Grade 7 student at A. M. Cunningham School, there arrived in our classroom a set of the recently published *Saga of a City*. It was this fascinating book, prepared by Mr. G. Milton Watson, a Hamilton principal, together with the inspiring way its contents were presented to us by our teacher, Mr. Harold B. Jackson, that awakened in me an interest in Hamilton's past. I am indebted to all the local historians, especially Mabel Burkholder, Marjorie Freeman Campbell, C. M. Johnston and T. R. Woodhouse, whose writings have since nurtured this interest. My appreciation is extended to Miss Dorothy Simpson and her capable staff in the Reference Department of the Hamilton Public Library for their courtesy and assistance to this frequent visitor.

I should like to thank Mr. P. W. Diebel, Assistant Superintendent of Public Schools, who acted as my mentor for this project and who attended to a number of its details for me. I am much obliged to Mrs. Betty Lorimer and her Dictapool staff at the Education Centre for typing the manuscript, and Miss M. Vail and Messrs. C. Crozier, L. A. Jeffery and J. C. Ruddle for proofreading it. My sincere gratitude is acknowledged to Mr. John

Nugent, Art Consultant, for the attractive cover design. Thanks are also owing to Mr. K. G. McLeod, principal of Burkholder School, to Mr. K. W. Wallace and some of his pupils for help in selecting a title and to Mrs. R. Leitch and the following pupils for the illustrations which appear in the book: Lynn Carter, Lynne Martyn, Philip Garcia, Mark Johnston, Richard Kowalchuk, Richard Lindstrom, Joseph Monaco and John Storrie.

Others to whom I am grateful for their assistance include the members of the advisory committee which helped to establish guidelines for this undertaking; Mrs. Gwen Metcalfe, Curator of Dundurn Castle; Mr. E. A. Simpson, City Clerk; Miss Lillian Shaw and Mr. Charles Doubrough of the Head-of-the-Lake Historical Society; Mr. Howard Cope, owner of the Ancaster Mountain Mills; Mr. Ron Mills of Westdale Secondary School; the staffs of the Education Centre Library, the Ontario Public Archives, the Baldwin Room of the Toronto Public Library and the library of the *Hamilton Spectator*; the Champlain Society, the Lundy's Lane Historical Society and the Ontario Historical Society for permission to quote from their publications; the many individuals and organizations that provided photographs and other illustrative material; and Mr. Campbell B. Hughes and the staff of the Ryerson Press for all their advice and help to this novice in the field of writing and publishing.

Lastly, I should like to thank my colleagues and friends for their interest and encouragement and my family for their patience and understanding. Without these throughout the past two and a half years, this book would never have become a reality.

March, 1969   L.C.E.

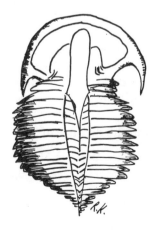

Contents

Maps

Bibliography

The General Bibliography lists those sources which cover a broad spectrum of Hamilton's growth. Histories of some of the neighbouring townships and municipalities are also included.

References dealing with specific aspects of the area's development are included in the sectional bibliographies which follow. Both primary and secondary sources are included.

General

Burkholder, Mabel, *The Story of Hamilton*, Hamilton, Davis-Lisson, 1938.

Burkholder, Mabel, *Barton on the Mountain*, Hamilton, 1956.

Burkholder, Mabel, *Out of the Storied Past*, Hamilton, 1968.

Campbell, Marjorie Freeman, *A Mountain and a City*, Toronto, McClelland and Stewart, 1966.

Cornell, John A., and the Beverly Township Centennial Committee, *The Pioneers of Beverly*, Centennial Edition, 1967.

Dick-Lauder, Mrs., and others, *Wentworth Landmarks*, Hamilton, Spectator Printing Co., 1897; reprinted, Toronto, Ryerson, 1967.

Emery, Claire and Ford, Barbara, *From Pathway to Skyway, A History of Burlington*, Burlington, Confederation Centennial Committee, 1967.

Hamilton Public Library, clipping files and scrapbooks.

Hamilton Spectator, 1846, on microfilm.

Hamilton Spectator, Centennial Edition, June 27, 1967.

Hamilton-Wentworth Planning Area Board, *An Atlas of the County of Wentworth*, Hamilton, City Hall, 1959.

Head-of-the-Lake Historical Society, *Wentworth Bygones*, No. I, (1958) to No. VII, (1967), Hamilton.

Jefferys, C. W., *The Picture Gallery of Canadian History*, 3 vol., Toronto, Ryerson, 1942, 1945, 1950.

Johnston, C. M., *The Head of the Lake, A History of Wentworth County*, Hamilton, 1958, 1967.

Mills, Stanley, *Lake Medad and Waterdown*, Hamilton, 1937.

Mundy, George A., *They Scattered the Seed, The Early History of Binbrook Township and Some of Its Churches*, Grimsby, 1967.

Page and Smith, *Illustrated Historical Atlas of the County of Wentworth*, Toronto, 1875.

Smith, J. H., *Historical Sketch of the County of Wentworth and the Head of the Lake*, Hamilton, 1897.

Stewart, Logan, *This Is Where I Live, The Saga of Hamilton, Canada*, Hamilton, Davis-Lisson, 1946.

Thomson, Thomas, *Hamilton City Sketches*, Hamilton, Board of Education for the City of Hamilton, 1954.

Waterdown East Flamborough Centennial Committee, *Waterdown and East Flamborough*, Hamilton, Griffin, 1967.

Watson, Milton, *Saga of a City*, Hamilton, 1947.

Wentworth Historical Society Papers and Records, Vol. I, (1892) to Vol. XI, (1924), Hamilton.

Wingfield, Alexander H. (ed.), *The Hamilton Centennial, 1846-1946*, Hamilton, Davis-Lisson, 1946.

Woodhouse, T. Roy, *The History of the Town of Dundas*, 3 parts, 1965, 1967, 1968.

Part I

. . . endowed by nature

YEARS AGO	
1,000,000,000	Precambrian bedrock of Ontario formed
500,000,000	warm inland seas flood Southern Ontario
	—layers of sediment gradually turn to rock
300,000,000	seas retreat
	—escarpment eroded from sedimentary rock
1,000,000	beginning of Ice Age
	—four periods of glaciation
12,000	final retreat of glaciers
	—Lake Iroquois and Niagara Falls appear
	high level bar ———— Dundas Marsh
	—Lake Ontario comes into being
	low level bar————Burlington Bay
6,000	man living in this area
	mastodon becomes extinct

1

The Niagara Escarpment

Great blocks and fallen masses of the limestone, which in many places is seen towering 200 feet above, lie scattered over the bottom of the gorge . . . .

Sir William Logan, 1863
(*Geology of Canada*, p. 14)

Hamilton's most distinctive natural feature is the 300-foot wall winding its way through the middle of the city. Residents of this area refer to it as "the mountain." So much is it a part of the local landscape that Hamiltonians are inclined to forget that it is not a mountain and it is not exclusively ours.

It is really an escarpment. Its eastern end lies in New York State near the city of Rochester and its western end in the State of Wisconsin. Between these two points it passes through Southern Ontario, from Queenston westward to Hamilton and then northward to the shores of Georgian Bay. It continues northwesterly to form the backbone of the Bruce Peninsula, dips beneath the waters of the bay and then emerges again to form Manitoulin Island and its neighbours. In some places along its 250-mile length it almost disappears from view; in others it rises majestically a thousand feet above the land below.

Had this wall been built by man, its origins would long ago have been recorded in legend and in fact. But it is to the geologist and paleontologist, rather than to the anthropologist and historian, that one must turn for the story of the formation of this ancient work of nature.

The foundation or bedrock of Southern Ontario is made up of the very ancient rocks of the Precambrian Shield. These rocks are estimated to be about 1,000 million years old. In Northern Ontario and in parts of Muskoka and Haliburton, these rocks appear on the earth's surface but in the rest of the province they are buried deeply beneath its surface.

3

In early Palaeozoic times (between 500 and 300 million years ago), much of Southern Ontario was flooded by warm inland seas. These seas swarmed with a great variety of invertebrate animal life. As these animals died, their remains accumulated on the floor of the seas. Gradually these remains and the impressions left by

THE NIAGARA ESCARPMENT

them became fossilized. From studying these fossils, paleontologists are able to tell what the animals were like. Some were microscopic in size; others were several inches long. Most had some form of shell rather than a skeleton to give them shape. Many bore a resemblance to snails, clams, crabs and other modern forms of shellfish. There were extensive coral reefs. Jellyfish were also thought to have been numerous but no evidence of these shell-less creatures remains.

To the east of these warm seas rose the young and rugged Appalachian Mountains. Numerous rivers flowed westward from these mountains down to the inland seas. They carried immense quantities of clay, silt, sand and other materials. Huge deltas formed where these materials were deposited. The heavier sands settled first. The finer silts and clays were carried further into the seas until they too were deposited. As movements within the earth caused the surface or crust to rise, the seas retreated. When subsequent movements caused the crust to sink, the seas advanced again. In this way, layer upon layer of sand, silt and calcareous material (the remains of the shellfish) built up on the underlying Precambrian bedrock.

ALBION FALLS
Notice the layers of sedimentary rock
and the talus at the base of the falls.

HUNTING FOR FOSSILS
The stratified layers of the escarpment
yield many interesting fossils.

As more and more layers were added, the pressure caused the individual particles of the lower layers to become "cemented" together into rock. This process is called lithification. Eventually the layers of sand became sandstone. The layers of clay and silt became shale rock. Lime from the animal remains and from the sea water formed limestone and dolomite. These are all known as sedimentary rocks. Colourful and interesting minerals sometimes crystallized within the cracks and crevices of the limestone and dolomite. Lithification continued until there was a covering of sedimentary rocks, thousands of feet thick, over the Precambrian rock.

The seas made their final retreat some 300 million years ago. Huge rivers drained what is now Southern Ontario. One such river is thought to have made its way in a northwesterly direction towards the present Georgian Bay basin. Another apparently flowed southeasterly into what is now the Lake Ontario basin. As these rivers crossed Southern Ontario, they gradually cut their way into the layers of sedimentary rock. The western bank was much more sharply eroded because of the general slope of the land. This steep bank became the face of the escarpment.

Water cut quickly into the soft underlying layers of sandstone and shale. When the harder overhanging limestone could no longer withstand this undercutting, it crashed to the level below. The face of the escarpment thus remained vertical. This continuing process is known as sapping. Huge piles of the fallen material called talus are found in many places at the foot of the escarpment.

Flowing into the huge ancient rivers were smaller tributaries. Deep ravines and valleys were cut where these fell over the edge of the escarpment. Today these form one of the escarpment's most attractive features. The Dundas Valley is a product of those times. A river which would have rivalled today's Niagara once made its way through the area cutting the valley as it did so.

Thus the general form of the escarpment was hewn . . . long, long before the dawn of recorded history and long before the great Ice Age when huge glaciers covered this area.

2

The Ice Age

*. . . we pursued our journey next day with the fatigue you may
imagine; sometimes in the water up to mid-leg . . . .*

Father Galinée's Narrative, 1669
(Coyne, *O.H.S. Papers and Records*, IV, p. 43)

Dramatic sculpturing of the local landscape continued during the
Ice Age which began about a million years ago. On four separate
occasions, huge glaciers slowly advanced out of the north burying
most of Canada and parts of the United States under a blanket of
ice and snow as much as two miles deep in some places. Most of
the evidence of the Ice Age that can be seen in this area belongs
to the last period of glaciation known as the Wisconsin.

As the glaciers bulldozed their way over the earth, they ploughed
and scraped and pushed. In many places this activity left only a
thin covering of soil over the sedimentary rock of the escarpment.
This is noticeable on top of the escarpment in the Hamilton area
where excavations for sewers and new homes frequently have to
be blasted out of the rock.

In some places the soil covering was completely removed. Such
outcroppings of bare rock are common in the Rockton area of
Beverly Township. Stones and boulders caught in the underside
of the glaciers sometimes chiselled deep scratches and grooves into
the outcroppings. These occur more or less in a northeast to southwest pattern, the direction in which the glaciers travelled.

Clay, sand and gravel were dumped by the glaciers into valleys
and ravines to an average depth of 75 to 100 feet. The Dundas
Valley contains considerable deposits of this unconsolidated drift
material. In some places, as in the Caledon Hills area near Orange-
ville, drift material even buried the brow of the escarpment.

Smooth, egg-shaped hills called "whalebacks" or drumlins were
formed during the forward movement of the glaciers. The ends

7

facing the direction from which the ice came are blunt whereas the other ends have long, gentle slopes. They are believed to have been formed from masses of clay material clinging to some nucleus such as a rock, then being shaped and smoothed by the ice sliding over them. Drumlins are usually found in groups. There are several rising to 100 feet and more in the Westover area. Because of poor drainage, the land amongst them tends to be swampy. Beverly Swamp lies close to the Westover drumlins.

As the glaciers began to melt they left behind the stones and boulders caught in them. These were often of rock foreign to this area such as granite and gneiss from the Precambrian Shield of Northern Ontario. These erratics were a nuisance to pioneer farmers. Some were used as building material for barn foundations and houses. Most were piled along the edges of fields to serve as fences. But no matter how many were picked up, a new crop of stones was exposed every spring.

The ice sheets did not melt back at a uniform rate. Wherever they rested for a period of time, deposits of drift material were left behind in the form of irregular rolling hills known as moraines. Morainic hills which contain a variety of clays, sands, gravels and

STONE FENCE   Large stones such as these were left behind by the retreating glaciers. They were a nuisance to pioneer farmers who often piled them along the edges of their fields to serve as fences.

A DRUMLIN NEAR WESTOVER

boulders are found above the escarpment between Dundas and Waterdown. They are also very common around Galt.

A section of the escarpment, through both preglacial and glacial erosion, sometimes became separated from the rest of the escarpment to form a flat-topped hill or mesa standing by itself. The largest, near Milton, is about four square miles in extent. Rattlesnake Point forms its southwest corner. Other similar formations appear as islands in Georgian Bay.

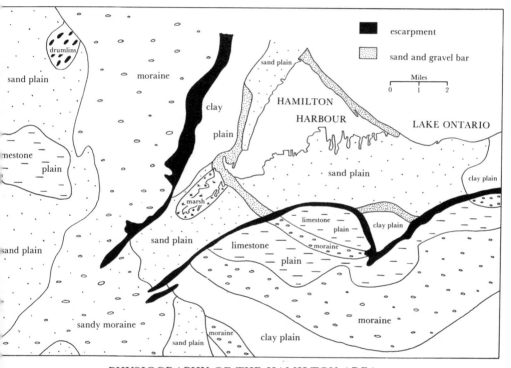

PHYSIOGRAPHY OF THE HAMILTON AREA

Caves exist in some parts of the escarpment. These were formed when water worked its way through cracks in the rock and dissolved away some of the material within. Cave exploration or spelunking is increasing in popularity. Several caves have been found in the Mount Nemo-Milton area and no doubt there are many more awaiting discovery. Short stalactites are found in some of them. William Lyon Mackenzie is alleged to have hidden in one of these caves during his flight from Toronto in 1837.

One of the best ways to study the geological history of this area is from the 450-mile Bruce Trail which follows the escarpment from the Niagara River to the tip of the Bruce Peninsula. As the trail traverses Hamilton, it hugs the stratified slopes of the escarpment. It winds for several miles across the rolling Dundas Valley. It then skirts Dundas Peak, Flamborough Head, Mount Nemo and Rattlesnake Point before heading northward. A walk along any section is a hike into our province's prehistoric past.

3

Lake, Bay and Marsh

A violent E. wind & terrible surf—a prodigious Sea this Eveng. I stood for some time under an Umbrella to admire its grandeur. . . .

Mrs. Simcoe's Diary, June 15, 1796

One of the major outcomes of the Ice Age was the emergence of the Great Lakes. Previously they had been only large valleys. These were widened and deepened by the advancing glaciers. When the glaciers withdrew, the gigantic hollows became filled with melt water. Because of the vast amount of water released by the melting glaciers, these early Great Lakes were much larger than their counterparts of today.

Lake Ontario in its ancestral form is known to geologists as Lake Iroquois. Traces of its shoreline still exist. Along the Scarborough bluffs near Toronto, it coincided with the present shore of Lake Ontario. In most places between the Niagara River and Trenton, however, its beaches were two to eight miles from those of today. Highway 8 between Queenston and Hamilton closely follows a bluff that was once lapped by the waters of Lake

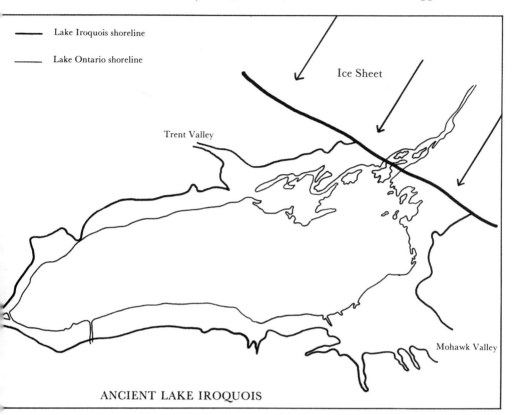

Lake Iroquois shoreline

Lake Ontario shoreline

Ice Sheet

Trent Valley

Mohawk Valley

ANCIENT LAKE IROQUOIS

Iroquois. Aldershot is built upon the beach of Lake Iroquois. Between Bronte and Oakville the ancient shoreline appears as a distinct terrace to the north of the Queen Elizabeth Highway.

Spill water from the early Great Lakes created connecting river systems. Water spilling over from ancient Lake Erie into Lake Iroquois became the Niagara River. As it tumbled over the escarpment at Queenston, the falls was formed. In the thousands of years that have since passed, the falls has eroded its way back to its present location some seven miles upstream. The scenic Niagara Gorge was created in the process.

At the western end of Lake Iroquois, the westward drift of the current aided by the wind carried sand and silt away from the

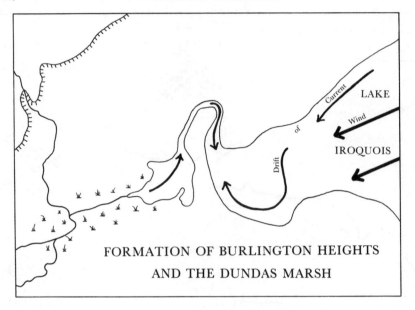

FORMATION OF BURLINGTON HEIGHTS
AND THE DUNDAS MARSH

north shore and deposited it along the south shore to form a plain between the base of the escarpment and the lake. Sediment deposited by streams flowing into Lake Iroquois helped to enlarge this plain. The area of the city today known as the Delta was once the mouth of such a stream.

The combined action of wind and current also caused the formation of a high gravelly bar across the lower Dundas Valley. This ridge of high ground, today known as Burlington Heights, caused the water from the creeks and streams flowing through the valley and into the lake to become partially impounded. This gave birth to the Dundas Marsh (Cootes Paradise).

Lake Iroquois drained into the ocean by way of the Mohawk Valley. After the weight of ice and snow had been removed from this area, the land slowly rose. A new outlet to the ocean by way of the St. Lawrence Valley was exposed. Lake Iroquois gradually shrank and Lake Ontario as we know it today came into existence. Another bar formed across the western end of the lake. Behind this low sandy bar, commonly known as the beach strip, Burlington Bay (Hamilton Harbour) appeared.

MASTODON SKELETON
(FROM WELLAND COUNTY)
The left tusk was knocked out
while the animal was very young and
only the right one developed.

Royal Ontario Museum

The building up of the plain on the south shore of the bay continued, the higher land near the base of the escarpment being the legacy of Lake Iroquois and the swampy, deeply-indented area near the bay shore being of more recent origin. It was on this plain that the city of Hamilton would one day grow.

Mammals had appeared on this continent by the time of the Ice Age. The bones of a large elephant-like creature known as the mastodon have been found in many parts of Southern Ontario including the Hamilton area. From these remains scientists are able to determine what the animal was like. It was about the size of an elephant and it had a flexible trunk. In addition to the two long ivory tusks projecting from the upper jaw, it also had a pair of short tusks which were possibly used to strip leaves and twigs from trees. The body is believed to have been covered with coarse, shaggy hair.

Evidence suggests that the mastodon survived the Ice Age by moving southward as the ice sheets advanced and returning to this area as the glaciers melted. As Southern Ontario became warmer and drier, the coniferous forests and swamps favoured by this beast disappeared. This probably led to the eventual dying out of the animal.

Bibliography

Part I (Geology)

Bruce Trail Association, *The Bruce Trail Guide Book*, Hamilton, 1965.

Bush, Helen, "Buried Treasure," *Canadian Audubon*, XXI, (November-December, 1959), pp. 163-166.

Bush, Helen, *Treasure in the Rock*, Toronto, Longmans, 1960.

Bush, Helen, "The Geological Story of the Niagara Escarpment," *Canadian Audubon*, XXV, (May-June, 1963), pp. 77-81.

Chapman, L. J. and Putnam, D. F., *The Physiography of Southern Ontario*, Toronto, University Press, 1951, 1966.

Johnson, William F., "The Historical Evolution of Hamilton Beach," *Wentworth Bygones*, II, (1960), pp. 31-35.

Judd, W. W. (ed.), *A Naturalist's Guide to Ontario*, Toronto, University of Toronto Press, 1964.

Mallory, E. S., "Bruce Trail," *Canadian Geographical Journal*, LXXI, (December, 1965), pp. 192-201.

Ontario Naturalist, The, IV, (December, 1966). Several articles about the Niagara Escarpment.

Royal Ontario Museum, *What? Why? When? How? Where? Who?* series, Toronto, University of Toronto Press.

    Lemon, R. R. H., *Fossils in Ontario*, 1965.

    Russell, L. S., *The Mastodon*, 1965.

    Tovell, Walter M., *The Niagara Escarpment*, 1965.

    Tovell, Walter M., *Niagara Falls: Story of a River*, 1966.

Watson, J. W., "Hamilton and its Environs," *Canadian Geographical Journal*, XXX, (May, 1945), pp. 240-252.

Part II

. . . Indian territory

c. 1570	formation of Iroquoian Confederacy (League of Five Nations)
1615	possible visit by Brulé to this area
1626	Father Daillon spends winter with Neutrals
1640	Fathers Brébeuf and Chaumonot attempt to establish mission amongst Neutrals
1650	Neutral Nation destroyed by Five Nations Confederacy
1669	La Salle visits western end of Lake Ontario
1678	trading post built by French at mouth of Niagara River (later Fort Niagara)
c. 1720	Tuscaroras join League of Five Nations
1742	birth of Thayendanegea (Joseph Brant)
1759	Fort Niagara captured by British; fall of New France
1775	outbreak of American Revolution
1784	land at Head of Lake Ontario purchased by British from Mississaugas
	Six Nations granted land along Grand River

4

The Attiwandaronks

Many prehistoric implements have been found near the Red Hill creek, which in the time of the Indians was a good salmon stream. Chipping places are found near many parts of its course, also small burial places containing one or two graves.

Frank Wood, 1915
(*W.H.S. Papers and Records*, VI, p. 11)

During the seventeenth century when the French were establishing themselves in North America, the area around the western end of Lake Ontario was inhabited by a large nation of Indians known to their Huron neighbours as the Attiwandaronks or "people of a slightly different language." It is generally thought that, because of the similarity of their way of life, they were part of the large Iroquoian family which also included the Hurons, the Petuns (Tobaccos) and the Five Nations Confederacy (Senecas, Cayugas, Onondagas, Oneidas and Mohawks).

The Attiwandaronks were known to the French as *Les Neutres* (the Neutrals), because they did not participate in the wars between their northern brethren of the Huron and Tobacco nations and their southern brethren of the Five Nations. Any Indian from one of the warring tribes had sanctuary while on Neutral soil.

At one time it was thought that the Neutrals did not engage in the Iroquoian wars because they made a good profit supplying flint from Lake Erie's shores to both sides for making weapons. Recent authorities, however, refute this idea for they say that flint was available to all the Iroquoian nations in their own areas.

It is thought more likely that the Neutrals did not want to take sides in the ongoing conflict for, situated as they were between the two warring groups, they did not want their territory turned into a battlefield. The Neutrals were, nevertheless, superior warriors and they did wage savage warfare on Algonkian tribes living in what is now Michigan and Illinois.

17

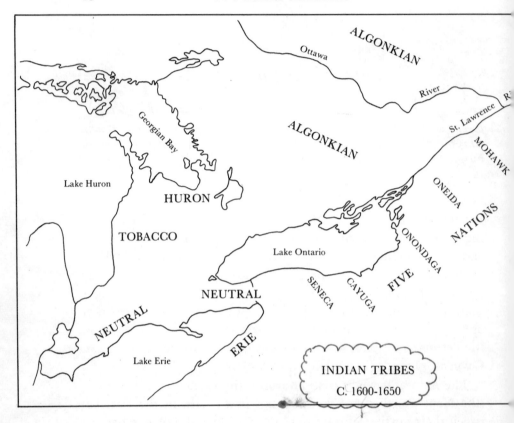

INDIAN TRIBES
C. 1600-1650

Some scholars say that the Attiwandaronks occupied that part of Ontario south of an imaginary line drawn approximately from where Toronto is situated on Lake Ontario to where Goderich now stands on the shore of Lake Huron. Others say that they were not spread over such a wide territory. They claim that the villages of the Attiwandaronks were concentrated between the Niagara River and the Grand River. A few may have been east of the Niagara River in what is now New York State.

Their chief village is thought by most authorities to have been on the bank of the Grand River somewhere in the vicinity of Brantford. King Street and Mohawk Road were once parts of trails that ran from it to the mouth of the Niagara River where there also was a large settlement. Another was on the shore of Lake

Medad near Waterdown. York Street in bygone times was possibly a portion of the trail leading to it. Evidence suggests that there was another large site in the Westover area. The Neutrals did not settle, however, on the swampy plain where the city of Hamilton now stands. They preferred to build on high defensible ground between valleys or in the loop of a stream.

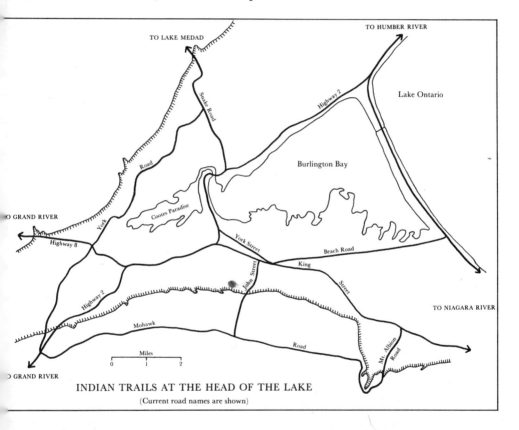

INDIAN TRAILS AT THE HEAD OF THE LAKE
(Current road names are shown)

Countless Indian artifacts have been collected in Wentworth and neighbouring counties. Several Neutral sites have been excavated. Relics unearthed on a typical dig include fragments of pottery vessels, implements and weapons made of bone and stone, beads and ceremonial objects. From a study of these remains, archaeologists and anthropologists are able to glean information about the living habits and customs of the Neutrals.

Hamilton Spectator

Watson's Studio, Midland

ARCHAEOLOGICAL INVESTIGATION   An Indian burial site in Beverly Township is studied by a team from McMaster University.

HURON INDIAN VILLAGE AT MIDLAND
The visitor has an intimate look at life in a typical Iroquoian village.

A typical Neutral village, like those of other Iroquoian Indians, was usually surrounded by a palisade. Inside it were a number of bark houses, each of which housed several families. The Neutrals were agriculturalists. Corn, tobacco, squash and beans were grown outside the palisade. Only when the fertility of the land in an area became exhausted did the Neutrals move to a new location.

The quantity of animal bones in their villages indicates that the Neutrals hunted and fished to supplement their agricultural food supply. Many hunting camps were located throughout their territory. Hunting weapons included arrow points of many shapes and sizes and spear heads. Some had serrated edges. War points were sometimes covered with rattlesnake poison. Skinning stones, scrapers and stone knives were used.

Several Indian burial places have also been discovered around Hamilton. After death occurred, a body was kept in the village, sometimes on a high scaffold, until all the flesh had decayed from the bones. The bones were then reverently displayed in the family's cabin. Every few years the Feast of the Dead was held at which time all the bones were gathered up and, with elaborate ceremony, placed in a common grave or ossuary.

Indian artifacts are still to be found in this area. Likely locations are freshly ploughed fields, along the banks of streams, around the base of uprooted trees and in the castings around animal holes, especially in areas where Indian artifacts have been previously found. Any large finds or anything of an unusual nature could be of historical significance and should be reported to McMaster University for professional investigation. Collections of Indian artifacts from this area can be studied in local museums. For an intimate look at life in a typical Iroquoian village, a visit to the reconstructed Huron village at Midland is an exciting experience.

5

Frenchmen Amongst the Neutrals

. . . I made them a present of what little I had, as little knives and other trifles, which they esteem highly. For in this country nothing is done with the Indians without making them some kind of present.

Father Daillon, 1627
(Johnston, *The Valley of the Six Nations,*
The Champlain Society, 1964, p. 4)

Supplementing the knowledge about the Neutrals gained from archaeological investigation and a study of their artifacts, there are contemporary accounts about their customs and living habits written by early explorers and missionaries of New France.

In 1615 Etienne Brulé made a trip from Huronia to the area south of Lake Erie. He made no known written records of his trip but from references to the Neutral nation which he is alleged to have made upon his return, historians have concluded that he must have passed around the western end of Lake Ontario through Neutral territory.

Champlain mentioned the Neutrals in the narrative of his journey to the Huron country. He mentioned that they produced great quantities of tobacco. He also recorded that they then numbered about 4,000 powerful warriors and lived in 40 populous villages. As he did not actually visit the Neutrals, it is quite probable that he learned of them from Brulé.

One who was inspired by these accounts of the Neutrals was Father de La Roche Daillon, a Récollet priest. In an attempt to introduce and spread Christianity amongst them, Daillon lived with the Neutrals during the winter of 1626-27. His experiences and observations were recorded in a letter to a friend in France.

On the sixth day of his travels from the land of the Petuns, he and his small party arrived at the first of the Neutral villages, thought to be that of Kandoucho on the shore of Lake Medad near Waterdown. He visited four others before reaching the village of Souharissen (also spelled Tsohahissen), powerful chief of the Neutral nation.

Daillon had much praise for the territory of the Neutrals:

There is an incredible number of stags . . . . There is also a great abundance of moose or elk, beaver, wild-cats and black squirrels larger than the French; a great quantity of wild geese, turkeys, cranes, and other animals, which are there all winter, which is not long and rigorous as in Canada . . . . the rivers furnish much excellent fish; the earth gives good grain, more than is needed. They have squashes, beans, and other vegetables in abundance . . . . .

(Johnston, p. 6)

He wrote of the fine physical condition of the Neutrals and of their prowess as warriors and hunters. He described one of their superstitions which required them to kill all animals they saw whether they needed them or not, lest they go and tell the other animals how they were being hunted.

The Hurons were not anxious for Daillon to work with the Neutrals. They did not want good relations between the French and Neutrals for this might lead to direct trade between them. The Hurons would then lose their profitable role as middlemen. The Hurons circulated rumours amongst the Neutrals that Daillon was a magician. Thus he came to be treated with suspicion and his work of introducing Christianity was greatly hindered. After only a few months he abandoned his mission and returned to Huronia.

Some thirteen years later, two Jesuit priests, Father Jean de Brébeuf and Father Joseph Marie Chaumonot, again attempted to establish a mission amongst the Neutrals. A report of their work appeared in *The Jesuit Relations*. Information about the Neutrals was also recorded:

They dress their pelts with much care and skill, and study to beautify them in many ways; but still more their own bodies, upon which, from the head even to the feet, they cause to be made a thousand different figures with charcoal pricked into the flesh, upon which previously they have traced their lines,—so that sometimes one sees the face and breast ornamented with figures . . . and the remainder of the body is appropriately decorated.

(Thwaites, *The Jesuit Relations*, p. 197)

Brébeuf and Chaumonot, like Daillon, found their work hampered by suspicion and hostility created by tales spread by the Hurons. During their brief sojourn, they visited several Neutral villages and gave them Christian names. They also did an extensive study of the Neutral language.

In addition to archaelogical investigation and contemporary accounts, a third source of information about Indian peoples is the legends and traditions of the people themselves. Unfortunately, little of the folklore of the Neutrals has survived for the Neutral nation ceased to exist over three hundred years ago.

After the Five Nations destroyed Huronia in 1648, they then turned against the Neutrals. Some say this was because the Neutrals offered shelter to some of the Hurons who escaped. Within a very few years the once-powerful Neutral nation had fallen before the savage onslaught of the Five Nations. The latter had acquired firearms from the white man, and against these the arrows and war clubs of the Neutrals were no match. Archaeological evidence indicates that a major battle took place in the Westover area. Tradition says that the decisive battle was fought on the shore of Hamilton Harbour at the foot of Emerald Street. The very few Neutrals who escaped slaughter likely fled or were adopted into the Five Nations. The mighty Attiwandaronks were no more.

The Senecas fell heir to the Neutral territory which they used only for hunting purposes.

6

Sieur de La Salle

We . . . at last, after five days' voyage, arrived at the end of Lake Ontario, where there is a fine large sandy bay, at the bottom of which is the outlet of another little lake discharging itself. This our guides made us enter about half a league . . . .

Father Galineé's Narrative, 1669
(Coyne, *O.H.S. Papers and Records*, IV, p. 41)

In the summer of 1669 a flotilla of seven canoes left Montreal. One of the leaders of the expedition was René Robert Cavelier, Sieur de La Salle. The goal of this 25-year-old adventurer was to discover and explore a great river (the Ohio), of which he had heard rumours, in the hope that it might lead to the Pacific Ocean. Also travelling with the party were two Sulpician priests, Father Casson and Father Galinée, who hoped to establish a mission amongst the Indians in the area southwest of Lake Erie. Father Galinée kept a detailed account of their journey.

After paddling up the St. Lawrence and along the south shore of Lake Ontario, they spent some time visiting with the Senecas of the Five Nations in an unsuccessful attempt to secure guides. They were advised, however, that guides might be obtained at a hunting village of their nation at the head of the lake. They then continued along the south shore past the mouth of the mighty Niagara River. Although Galinée gave an accurate description of the falls, they did not take time to see it.

They entered the little lake (Burlington Bay) at the end of Lake Ontario and set foot on its shores, the first white men ever recorded to have done so. Careful study of Galinée's journal has led to the conclusion that their landing was in the vicinity of today's La Salle Park. The village of Tinawatawa (Tinaouatoua) that they were seeking lay several miles inland. They camped on the shore and waited for a delegation from the village to escort them there.

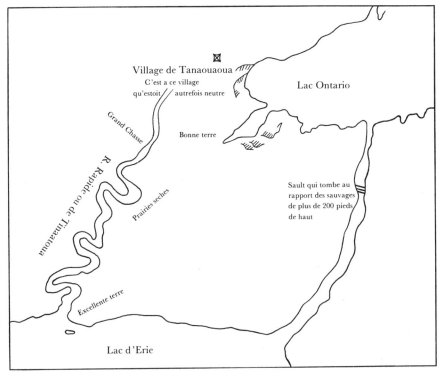

GALINÉE'S MAP OF 1669

While waiting, La Salle went hunting and returned to the camp with a high fever. Father Galinée wrote of it:

Some say it was at the sight of three large rattlesnakes he found in his path whilst climbing a rock that the fever seized him. It is certainly, after all, a very ugly sight; for these animals are not timid like other serpents, but wait for a man, putting themselves at once in a posture of defence, coiling half the body from the tail to the middle as if it were a cable, holding the rest of the body quite erect, and darting sometimes as much as three or four paces, all the time making a great noise with the rattle that they carry at the end of their tails. There are a great many of them at this place, as thick as one's arm, six or seven feet long, entirely black. The rattle that they carry at the end of the tail, and shake very rapidly, makes a noise like that which a number of melon or squash seeds would make, if shut up in a box.

(Coyne, p. 41)

After three days, some fifty Indians came to meet them. Gifts were exchanged. The white men's were payment for the transport of their baggage and the purchase of two slaves. The gifts of the Indians, which included several dressed deer skins and about 5,000 wampum beads, were to ensure that the white men would do them no harm. They agreed to take the Frenchmen to their village whence they could proceed to the bank of a large river (the Grand) that flowed into Lake Erie.

They set out for Tinawatawa. The portage "sometimes in the water up to mid-leg" took two days. They are thought to have followed the course of Grindstone Creek to its headwaters in Beverly Swamp. Tinawatawa has been placed by scholars in the vicinity of Westover.

Upon their arrival at the village, they were surprised to find there another Frenchman by the name of Joliet. He had been on an expedition to the land of the Ottawas in the vicinity of the upper Great Lakes in search of a fabled copper mine. He had failed to find the mine and was returning to Montreal by way of the lower lakes, a route not previously known to the French.

The two priests made preparations to continue their journey, changing their proposed route to follow the one taken by Joliet. La Salle decided not to go on with them, claiming that the state of his health did not permit him to continue. He also said that

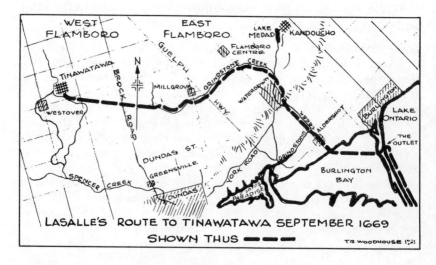

LASALLE'S ROUTE TO TINAWATAWA SEPTEMBER 1669
SHOWN THUS ▬ ▬ ▬

he did not want to subject his inexperienced men to a winter in the woods. Many historians feel, however, that La Salle was looking for an excuse to part company with the priests.

The two priests departed on their altered course. Their trip and that of Joliet were of significance for they proved the existence of a water route from Montreal to Lake Superior by way of Lake Ontario and Lake Erie, the route of today's great Seaway.

There exists no record of La Salle's subsequent direction. He may have spent the winter trading with the Senecas around Lake Ontario. Some biographers claim that he pushed on into the Ohio country south of Lake Erie in his quest for the western sea. However, it is possible that he merely made his way back to Montreal, having had initiation enough on his first expedition into the wilderness.

For the next hundred years there is little record of white men's activities at the western end of Lake Ontario. French missionaries probably continued their efforts among the Indians in the area. The French built a large trading post at the mouth of the Niagara River (Fort Niagara) and a smaller one at the mouth of the Humber where Toronto now stands. The Indians of this area undoubtedly made their way to these posts. Perhaps a trader occasionally visited their camps. The remains of European trade goods have been found in many local Indian sites.

Eventually the Senecas abandoned the area and drew back across the Niagara River. The Mississaugas, a nomadic Algonkian tribe, then moved in.

After New France fell to the British in 1759, little changed hereabouts except that the Union Jack replaced the fleur-de-lis on the flagpoles over the trading posts. It was not until the guns of the American Revolution had been silenced some twenty-five years later that white men came to the Head of the Lake with settlement as their intent.

Bibliography

Part II (Indians)

Coyne, James H., "The Country of the Neutrals," *Historical Sketches of the County of Elgin*, St. Thomas, The Elgin Historical and Scientific Institute, 1895, pp. 1-31.

Coyne, James H. (ed.), "Galinée's Narrative," *Ontario Historical Society Papers and Records*, IV, (1903), Toronto, pp. 3-75.

Dick-Lauder, Mrs., and others, *Wentworth Landmarks*, Hamilton, Spectator Printing Co., 1897; Toronto, Ryerson, 1967, pp. 74-91.

Jenness, Diamond, *Indians of Canada*, Ottawa, Queen's Printer, 1963 (6th edition), pp. 288-307.

Johnston, Charles (ed.), *The Valley of the Six Nations*, Toronto, The Champlain Society, 1964, pp. xxvii-xxxii, 3-34.

Martin, Kirwan, "The Neutral Nation," *Wentworth Historical Society Papers and Records*, VI, (1915), pp. 25-28.

Osler, E. B., *La Salle*, Don Mills, Longmans, 1967.

Ridley, Frank, *Archaeology of the Neutral Indians*, Etobicoke Historical Society, 1961.

Terrell, John Upton, *La Salle, The Life and Times of an Explorer*, Toronto, Clarke, Irwin & Co., 1968.

Thwaites, Reuben Gold (ed.), *The Jesuit Relations and Allied Documents*, XXI, Cleveland, Burrows Brothers, 1898, pp. 187-237.

Wood, Frank, "Indian Relics and Implements," *Wentworth Historical Society Papers and Records*, VI, (1915), pp. 5-16.

Woodhouse, T. Roy, "Route of La Salle & Galinée to Tinawatawa," unpublished manuscript, Hamilton Public Library.

Part III

. . . . at the Head
of the Lake

c. 1785	Loyalist settlers take up land at western end of Lake Ontario
1791	Barton Township surveyed by Augustus Jones
	Wilson and Beasley build mill at Ancaster
1792	Lake Geneva renamed Burlington Bay
1793	Governor Simcoe passes through area
	Militia Act
	first white child born at the Head of the Lake (Henry Beasley)
1794	King's Head Inn
1795	Barton Lodge meets at Smith's tavern
	Beasley appointed justice of the peace
1796	first school at the Head of the Lake (in Ancaster)
	visit by Simcoes to this area
	first crown patents issued in Barton Township
1800	Beasley offers property on Burlington Heights for sale
1801	Methodists hold services in home of Richard Springer
1806	Burlington Board of Agriculture

7

The Coming of the Loyalists

Neither confiscation of their property, the pitiless persecution of their kinsmen in revolt, nor the galling chains of imprisonment could break their spirits or divorce them from a loyalty almost without parallel.

Inscription, U.E.L. Monument,
Prince's Square, Hamilton

Two young men, Charles Depew, and his brother-in-law, George Stewart, according to family tradition, beached their canoe one autumn day in 1785 on the eastern end of the narrow strip of land separating Lake Ontario from the beautiful bay at the head of the lake. They dragged their canoe across the sand strip and continued their paddling along the south shore of the bay. They entered a large inlet near the foot of what is now Ottawa Street and went ashore.

There they claimed a sizeable portion of land for Charles' father, John Depew, by driving a stake bearing his name into the ground. George Stewart similarly marked a tract for himself about a mile to the west. They then got back into their canoe and returned whence they had come. What had brought these two to claim land in the unsettled wilderness at the head of the lake?

The story began several years earlier and hundreds of miles away when thirteen of Britain's colonies in North America revolted and demanded their independence. There were many people in those thirteen colonies, however, who refused to give their support to the struggle. Some were quite content with things as they had been and did not want changes made. Others were prevented by their strong feelings of loyalty towards Britain from taking up arms against her. Still others were forbidden by their religion from taking part in armed conflict. Some were wealthy and others were poor. Some owned vast estates but others owned no property. Some were well educated, whereas others could not read or write.

To the British they were "Loyalists"; to their discontented neighbours they were traitors. They were persecuted. They lost their right to vote. Their property and belongings were taken from them. Many were imprisoned. Some were even hanged. Some of the menfolk joined or helped the British forces but this caused their families to suffer greater persecution.

Flight was their alternative. They fled carrying what few possessions they were able to save. Some made their way to New York and other ports along the Atlantic coast to await transport on British ships to Britain, the West Indies, the Maritimes or up the St. Lawrence River to Quebec. Others followed overland routes northward and westward to Quebec. Many, especially from New York and Pennsylvania, made their way to Fort Niagara on Lake Ontario at the mouth of the Niagara River.

LOYALISTS ON THEIR WAY TO UPPER CANADA

C. W. Jefferys, Imperial Oil Collection

American forces had been unable to take this stronghold from the British. Under the protection of the fort's walls and guns the Loyalists sought refuge. Thousands came, weary and hungry and poorly clothed. The more fortunate came by boat, on horseback, by ox cart, or by Conestoga wagon. But most of them came on foot. In crude shelters they rested and waited. Most of them expected that Britain would soon regain her control over the rebellious colonies and they could then return to their homes.

Those in charge of the fort had the responsibility of providing food for all these people. A strip of land four miles wide on the western bank of the river was purchased from the Mississauga Indians. Some of the Loyalists were permitted to cross the river and farm this land. John Depew and his family were amongst them. But the land did not belong to them. Anything they grew that they did not need for their own family had to be sent to the fort.

As it became apparent that Britain had lost the struggle and that there would be no welcome for these Loyalists in the new United States of America, the British authorities had to make provision for them. Some reward for their loyalty and suffering was in order. More land was purchased from the Mississaugas in 1784. This purchase extended from the Niagara frontier to beyond the western end of Lake Ontario. The head of every Loyalist family could claim 200 acres. Extra acreage was often granted for military service. Former officials and army officers received the best lots and those closest to the Niagara River were chosen first. Most of the Loyalists had to go further into the wilderness to make their claims. This brought Charles Depew and George Stewart to the head of Lake Ontario on that autumn day in 1785.

They returned to Niagara for the winter. But as soon as possible they moved with their familes to their new property. Were they the first white settlers in this area? Some evidence suggests that they were. Other evidence indicates that Robert Land or Richard Beasley settled here before them. Local historians do not agree. However, the significant thing is that for the first time since the Neutrals were wiped out, there were settlers at the western end of Lake Ontario.

8

Robert Land, United Empire Loyalist

. . . your Petitioner came into Niagara as an express from Gen. Sir Henry Clinton in the Year one thousand seven hundred and seventy-nine—previous to which he had been employed in carrying expresses for the british army for two years, during which period his sufferings, and dangers were necessarily great and once after long confinement and condemnation he made his escape.

Petition of Robert Land, June 6, 1794
(Cruikshank, *O.H.S. Papers and Records*, XXIV, p. 84)

The story of Robert Land and his family vividly illustrates the suffering so often experienced by the Loyalists. Here is their story essentially as it was recorded by a great-grandson, John H. Land.

Before the Revolution, Land, his wife and their several sons and daughters lived on the bank of the Delaware River in the colony of New York. Robert Land owned a large and prosperous farm there. He was also a magistrate for the local area.

Land offered his services to the British upon the outbreak of hostilities. Because of his intimate knowledge of the surrounding countryside, he was employed in gathering information and carrying despatches. Most of his neighbours, however, supported the colonies in their struggle against Britain. To them Land was a traitor and a spy. His eldest son, John, being of military age, was seized and detained in prison throughout the conflict. The rest of the family had to suffer the insults and abuses of their former neighbours as they struggled to keep up the farm.

Bitterness grew. A group of local residents planned to disguise themselves as Indians and rid the area entirely of the Lands and another family by the name of Kane. On the chosen night, how-ever, 16-year-old Kate Land was awakened by a voice telling her that she was wanted at the Kanes' house across the river. She dressed hastily and paddled over in her canoe. Upon entering their door, she stumbled over the body of Mr. Kane. A hurried search revealed that the whole family had been murdered.

She quickly re-crossed the river and as she stepped ashore, the same voice warned her, "House burn, get children out." She roused the members of her family and as they crouched hidden in a cornfield, they watched their home burn to ashes. They then made their way to New York City which was under the protection of British troops.

Who had warned Kate in the night? Was it a friendly Indian who knew what was astir? Might it have been one of the raiding party who, although opposed to the venture, felt that for his own safety he had to go along?

Sometime thereafter, Robert Land's duties brought him into the area. He risked a visit to his home. The blackened ruins convinced him that his family had been killed. He made up his mind to leave the area at once and for all time. A Quaker friend, Ralph Morden, undertook to guide him to the Niagara River. Land's presence in the area became known, however, and a posse was sent after them. Morden gave himself up, confident that they would do him no harm as he had never taken up arms. But he was later hanged for his part in helping Land to escape.

Land fled with the members of the posse in pursuit. Just as he reached the edge of a thick woods, they let loose a volley of shots. They saw Land stumble and when they arrived at the spot they found a trail of blood leading into the woods. Darkness was descending. They assumed that Land had been mortally wounded and gave up the chase.

But the bullet had only struck his knapsack. The force of the impact had made him stumble. He cut his hand on a sharp stone causing the trail of blood. Travelling mostly under the cover of night, he slowly made his way northwest to Fort Niagara.

He received a grant of land near the falls, where he lived for two years. But it is said that the "solemn dirge" of the falls was more than he could bear so he moved to the head of Lake Ontario. He built himself a shanty (near the southwest corner of today's Barton and Leeming Streets) and sought comfort in the solitude of the wilderness, where he supported himself mainly by hunting and trapping.

Meanwhile, Loyalist families continued to flock to New York

City for refuge. Mrs. Land might have heard of her husband's assumed death from one of them. Finally the British had to evacuate the city and many of the refugees, including the Lands, were transported to New Brunswick.

They remained there for seven years but things did not go well for them. Robert, the youngest son, finally persuaded them to try their luck in Upper Canada. They travelled inland by way of New York State and stopped en route at their old home. John Land had been allowed to keep the family farm after being released from prison. He tried without success to get them to stay with him. They reached Niagara and settled there. The boys supported the family by hunting and trapping and by working for fellow settlers.

One day they chanced to hear of a white man with the same name as theirs living at the head of Lake Ontario. Curious, but trying not to let their hopes build, they undertook the forty-mile walk. One can imagine the joyful reunion that took place!

Robert Land eventually received title to over three hundred acres of land. With his sons' help, a prosperous farm developed. A fine homestead replaced the humble cabin. In time the sons received land grants of their own, adjacent to those of their father.

9

A New Life

*They prepared me some refreshment at this House, some excellent
Cakes baked on the Coals; Eggs; a boiled black squirrel; tea; & Coffee
made of Peas which was good, they said Chemists Coffee was better.
The sugar was made from black Walnut Trees which looks darker
than that from the Maple, but I think it is sweeter.*

Mrs. Simcoe's Diary, June 12, 1796

On the heels of Robert Land, Richard Beasley, the Depews
and the Stewarts, came other Loyalist families to take up land
grants at the Head of the Lake. Every family had its own story to
tell—a story of suffering and hardship.

Nor were their hardships ended upon their arrival here. Shelter
and food for the family had to be provided. Hands that had known
other skills had to wield an axe and push a plough. How else was
a man to support his family in the wilderness?

With little more than a hand axe to help him, the head of the
family soon erected a crude log shanty or shelter. The family then
undertook the task of clearing the land. Fortunate was the man
with several husky sons to assist him. Sometimes only the underbrush was cleared and a ring cut through the bark of the larger
trees which were then left standing until they died. Another
method was to cut the trees, drag them into piles, let them dry and
then burn them. The ashes were used to make potash which could
be sold or traded for goods they needed. But land clearing was
strenuous and slow. A settler was doing well to clear ten acres a
year.

Generally the land on top of the escarpment was more easily
cleared than that on the plain below. The shallow soil on the
higher level did not support as heavy a growth of trees. Clearing
on the lower level was further impeded by the numerous swampy
areas. Rattlesnakes which abounded in this area added to the
dangers of land clearing.

The land amongst the stumps was ploughed and seed was sown.

AN EARLY SETTLER'S HOME   REMAINS OF A STUMP FENCE

This is one of two pioneer log cabins on view at the Ball's Falls Conservation Area near Jordan.

Often only hand tools, many of which the settler made himself, were used. Many months and even years of labour were required before a family harvested a few bushels of surplus wheat which could be taken to the nearest post for a little cash or credit. Eventually the stumps were removed either by burning or blasting or by dragging them out with oxen. These were sometimes hauled to the edge of the fields and turned on their side to make fences.

Once the clearing and planting were underway, the head of the family could turn his attention to building a better home for his family. Logs were cut to size and trimmed. Neighbours helped to erect them into place. Doors and windows were cut out after the walls were up. A roof of elm bark or cedar shingles kept out the rain. The old shanty became a storage building or a small barn.

The new cabin which might be as much as twenty feet long and eighteen feet wide, usually had only one or two rooms within. There was sometimes a loft overhead where the children slept. The inside walls might be smoothed and a floor of thick boards laid. A fireplace was needed for lighting, cooking and heating.

The settlers made most of their furniture themselves. It was built to be useful rather than decorative. Even the cooking and eating utensils were handmade. Some families were able to bring one or two pieces with them from their former home—a favourite chair, perhaps, or a clock or a fine carved chest. Such a piece was given a place of prominence in their new dwelling.

The British government, in its desire to assist the Loyalist refugees, provided them with basic rations for three years. They were given flour, pork, a limited amount of beef, some butter and a little salt, as well as wheat, peas, corn and potatoes which were to be used for seed. Unfortunately for many families, their three years expired in 1788, the same year that severe drought caused widespread crop failure in Upper Canada. Great was the suffering in the hungry year that followed.

Generally, however, the Loyalists had enough to eat, even though it lacked much variety. Pork which was preserved in salt was the basic meat. This was supplemented with fish and game when there was time for such pursuits as fishing and hunting. Flocks of passenger pigeons were so thick that they were knocked from the trees with sticks or killed with clubs as they flew low.

The settlers at first had to grind their own wheat. This produced very coarse flour which made heavy, dark bread. Corn was easier to grind and cornmeal was used in many dishes. Potatoes were consumed in large quantities but few families took the time to grow other vegetables. Wild plants were used occasionally as vegetables and to make medicines. Wild fruits and berries were made into pies and puddings. Apples and pumpkins were grown. Wild honey or maple sugar was used for sweetening.

Tea was rarely available so substitutes made from such things as hemlock and sassafras were common. The men generally preferred beer, rum and whiskey which were plentiful and cheap. Milk and butter were scarce because few families had enough feed to keep cattle over the winter. Too frequently, bears ate their pigs and wolves gobbled up their sheep.

Many of the Loyalists had fled from the Thirteen Colonies with little more than the clothes they were wearing. These did not last long on a pioneer farm. More practical clothing of buckskin and homespun (linen and wool) replaced them.

Not all who received land grants at the lakehead settled on them. Many grants were sold to incoming settlers who were not Loyalists. Gradually the population at the Head of the Lake grew and, acre by acre, the wilderness was tamed.

10

Richard Beasley, Esquire

. . . we mounted our sleas and drove on to the house of a Mr. Baisley,
who keeps a shop at the head of the Lake Geneva, and trades much
with the Indians in peltry. . . .

Patrick Campbell, 1792
(*Travels in North America,*
The Champlain Society, 1937, p. 160)

While most of his fellow settlers were busy clearing and planting,
Richard Beasley was engaged in other pursuits which brought him
a position of leadership at the Head of the Lake.

He was born and raised near Albany, New York. When hostilities broke out in the Thirteen Colonies he joined a Loyalist ranger
corps. He was captured by the enemy. It is not known whether he
was released or escaped, but in 1777 this sixteen-year-old veteran
arrived in Niagara. There he served for two years as assistant
commissary or storekeeper for the British forces of that area.

He then became engaged in a trading venture. He and his partner established trading posts near the western end of Lake Ontario
and in the Toronto area. Their customers were the Mississauga
Indians who roamed these areas. Goods and credit were extended
to Beasley and his partner by the leading wholesale merchants of
the day, one of whom was Beasley's cousin.

Beasley was granted land at the Head of the Lake near today's
Main Street and Paradise Road, an area still known to city oldsters
as Beasley's Hollow. He took up residency there.

Later he took possession of the lands on the bay front where
Dundurn Park is now situated. He built a wharf and storehouse
at the water's edge and continued his trading activities. Nearby
Burlington Heights was a popular camping spot of the Mississauga
Indians. The Indians of the Six Nations also came to trade at
Beasley's post for it was adjacent to the trail from the Head of the
Lake to their reserve on the Grand River. The early white settlers
no doubt also came to Beasley's to exchange a few barrels of potash

INDIAN TRADING FURS, 1785
Richard Beasley's trading post
on Burlington Heights was likely
similar to the one shown here.

or a few bushels of surplus wheat for a supply of those few things such as tea, spices, sugar, cotton, powder and shot which they could not produce for themselves.

In 1791 Beasley undertook a new enterprise. He and James Wilson built a saw and grist mill on a stream flowing into the head of Cootes Paradise. This too was a boon to their fellow settlers. The closest mill had previously been at the Forty (Grimsby).

In the meantime, romance had come into Beasley's life. One day when he was riding through the willow thickets on the edge of Cootes Paradise, he came upon young Henrietta Springer. She had been taken from her home at the foot of the escarpment by a band of Indians but she had made her escape from them. Love blossomed between her and Beasley and they were married.

Lieutenant-Governor Simcoe twice visited with Beasley. In 1793 the governor and his party stopped overnight at Beasley's on their way back to Niagara following a tour of the western part of the province. Three years later both the governor and Mrs. Simcoe paid the Beasleys a visit and stayed to dine with them. Mrs. Simcoe praised the fine setting of Beasley's home in her diary.

Through grants and purchases, Beasley gradually acquired extensive holdings of land. By 1800 he owned hundreds of acres at the Head of the Lake and thousands of acres on the upper reaches of the Grand River. His intention was to sell the land to incoming settlers and make a considerable profit for himself.

Beasley undertook many of his business ventures on credit, usually to his cousin, Richard Cartwright. Repeatedly Cartwright had to press for payment of these debts. On one occasion Beasley was forced to put his property at Burlington Heights up for sale. But by one means or another, he always managed to raise enough money to calm his creditors and stay out of debtors' prison. Although he was much criticized for the manner in which he conducted some of his land deals, men like him who were willing to take financial chances played an important role in the development of Upper Canada.

In 1795 Beasley was appointed a justice of the peace and the next year a magistrate. This made him a member of the local Court of Quarter Sessions of the Peace which, in addition to trying criminal cases, enacted legislation, levied taxes and granted licences. It was also responsible for local public works and the erection of public buildings.

Beasley was elected to represent this area in the Legislative Assembly. He later served as its Speaker. In 1804 he was appointed to the élite Legislative Council of Upper Canada.

As was required of all able males, he enrolled in the local militia unit, the 2nd York Regiment. He later became its commanding officer.

Merchant, mill owner, militiaman, land magnate, magistrate, assemblyman and legislative councillor—Richard Beasley was indeed one of the leading citizens of his day at the Head of the Lake.

11

Thayendanegea

He is attended by two negroes; has established himself in the English way; has a garden and a farm; dresses after the European fashion; and nevertheless possesses much influence over the Indians.

Duke de La Rochefoucauld Liancourt, 1799
(*Travels*, I, p. 252)

Of all the early settlers at the Head of the Lake, none was more renowned than Thayendanegea, or Joseph Brant, as he was known to his white brethren. He was born a full-blooded Mohawk in an Indian hunting camp on the banks of the Ohio River. His older sister married Sir William Johnson who was the superintendent of Indian affairs in the colony of New York. Johnson took an active interest in his young brother-in-law and sent him to the Moor Charity School for Indians in Lebanon, Connecticut. Brant left the school after a few years to take part in the Pontiac Wars.

By 1765 he was living in the valley of the Mohawk River, the traditional home of his people. He married a chieftain's daughter and a son and daughter were born to them. He acquired land and cattle and a share in a grist mill. He translated the Gospel of St. Mark into the Mohawk tongue for his people. He became the chief of the Mohawks, the leading tribe of the Six Nations Confederacy. This peaceful and comfortable life was upset by the death of his wife from tuberculosis. He then married her half-sister but she too died from the disease.

Meanwhile, relations between Britain and her American colonies were becoming very strained. The Indians of the Six Nations were concerned about their position in the conflict that was brewing. Joseph Brant went to England on behalf of his people to seek information there. He was well received in court circles. This intelligent and majestic gentleman in no way fulfilled most Englishmen's impression of the typical North American savage.

By the time he returned home, the Revolution had started. Brant and the majority of his Six Nations tribesmen sided with

43

44

PORTRAIT OF JOSEPH BRANT
by William von Moll Berczy
The National Gallery of Canada, Ottawa

JOSEPH BRANT'S HOUSE
Reconstructed on its original site at
the western end of the beach strip,
it houses a fine museum featuring
the Indian life of this area.

the British. He teamed his warriors with Butler's famed Rangers and together from Fort Niagara, they made lightning raids upon settlements in the Mohawk and Ohio valleys. Many tales have been told about the unchecked cruelty of Brant and his warriors in these raids, but these have since been questioned by reputable authorities.

After the conflict ended the Indians expected, and deserved to receive, the same compensation as the white Loyalists. They had lost their ancestral homes in the Mohawk valley. Promises were made but the peace treaty between Britain and United States made no provision for the Indians. Brant reminded Britain of her forgotten promises and in 1784 a grant was made to the Mohawks and any others of the Six Nations who wished to settle there. This grant extended for six miles on each side of the Grand River from its mouth to its source.

Brant also received a considerable sum of money as compensation for his own property losses. He used this money to help his people get established. He bought tools, equipment and stock and built a saw mill for them. He translated the Book of Common Prayer into Mohawk. Gradually his people settled to life in their new homes.

The Indians realized they had more land than they needed and wanted to sell parts of it to white settlers. They planned to use the money to buy equipment and farm animals and to establish financial security for themselves. Brant thought it would be a good influence to have white settlers living amongst them.

But unlike other Loyalists, the Indians did not receive formal ownership of their grant. They were not permitted to sell any of it without the approval of the governor. This, it was said, was to prevent the Indians from being done out of their property by unscrupulous land grabbers. Brant again went to London, this time to secure the deed to the lands on the Grand River. His visit was a personal social triumph. He was entertained in aristocratic homes, had several outings with the Prince of Wales and was presented to the king and queen. But he failed to get the deed.

Brant continued to act as agent for his people in land negotiations. Affairs became so legally entangled that the Indians never did receive the true value for their property. Critics accused Brant of personal gain at the expense of his Indian brethren but this has never been proven.

After seeing his people established on the Grand River, Brant settled on a large grant at the western end of the Burlington Bay sand strip. He had married again during the Revolution. His third wife was the beautiful daughter of the head chief of the Turtle tribe, the most powerful of the Mohawk nation. It was she who had the power to designate the successor to the chieftaincy.

Brant built a large two-storied frame house facing a sheltered pond on the bay side of the sand strip at a time when most of his white neighbours still lived in log cabins. In this home Brant lived the life of a country gentleman. He had taken a number of Negro slaves as captives during the Revolution and these he retained in his service.

He was an honoured citizen in the local community. Across the bay on Burlington Heights was the home of Richard Beasley where he often dined. Brant's children were educated in the ways of the white man. But he did not forsake his Indian brethren. He continued to devote his life to securing recognition and opportunity for his people. Their canoes were often drawn up on the shore in front of his house. Hospitality was extended equally to Indian and white man.

One incident, however, marred his happiness. His eldest son, Isaac, was a difficult young man of violent disposition. He was very jealous of his father's third wife and his step-brothers and step-sisters. One night while Brant was visiting with Beasley, word was brought to him that Isaac was creating a disturbance in a nearby inn. Brant went to quell him. Isaac pulled a knife and in the scuffle which followed, Brant inflicted a shallow wound on his son's head. Refusing treatment, Isaac suffered infection and died. Brant insisted that he be tried for what he had done and, although he was acquitted by both the white man's court and the Six Nations Council, he never forgave himself for his son's death.

In 1807 the great chief died. The bell of the Mohawk Chapel beside the Grand River where he was laid to rest tolled for twenty-four hours. His wife chose their youngest son, John, to take his father's place as chief. Their daughter, Elizabeth, carried on her father's work of translating portions of the New Testament into the language of their people.

12

Development at the Head of the Lake

*I was born near the bay shore about two miles east of the city in
1798, and I can remember back to 1803.*

. . . .

*There were no schools here. I was sent to Niagara when I was eight
years old for one year at school, all I ever got.*

John Ryckman
(Woodhouse, *Wentworth Bygones*, v, p. 24)

When the Loyalists first came to this province, it was part of
Quebec. The region west of the Ottawa River was divided into
four districts. The area about the Head of the Lake was in the
District of Nassau.

One who had a considerable hand in the shaping of this district
was Augustus Jones, a land surveyor. One of his first assignments
was to survey a line northwesterly from the outlet on the beach
strip to define the area purchased from the Mississaugas in 1784.
It later became the Wentworth-Halton county line. He also surveyed the Indian lands on the Grand River to determine their
limits.

He assisted with the surveying of fifteen townships between the
Niagara River and the Head of the Lake. Number Seven was later
named Saltfleet because of the salt deposits discovered there. Immediately to the south of it was Binbrook. Number Eight was
renamed Barton. Between it and the Indian lands, Glanford was
later laid out. On the north shore of Lake Ontario a township
then called Geneva but later called East Flamborough was defined.

In his survey of Barton Township, Jones started with a base line
near the bay shore. The other three boundaries of this rectangular
township were then determined. Side roads running north and
south were placed half a mile (forty chains) apart. Concession
roads were marked every five-eighths of a mile (fifty chains), at
right angles to the side roads. This divided the township into
blocks and determined the limits of the land grants already

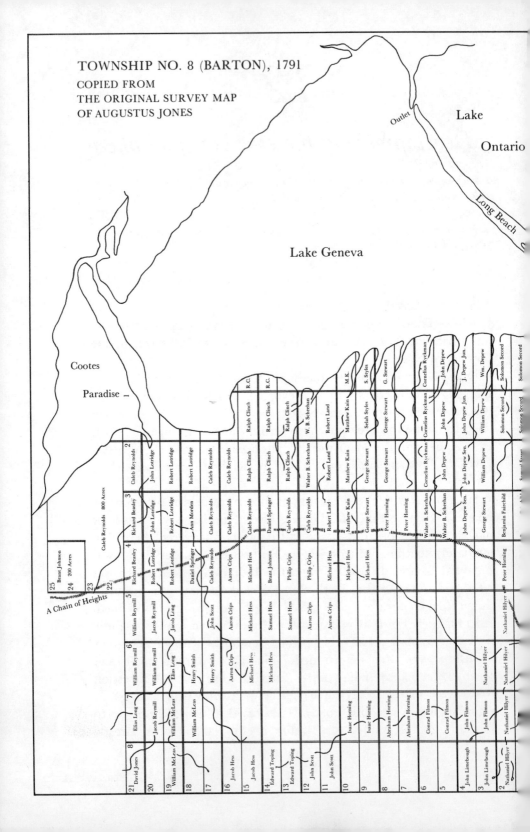

TOWNSHIP NO. 8 (BARTON), 1791

COPIED FROM
THE ORIGINAL SURVEY MAP
OF AUGUSTUS JONES

Lake
Ontario

Outlet

Long Beach

Lake Geneva

Cootes

Paradise —

A Chain of Heights

claimed. Each block contained two 100-acre lots. On his 1791 map of the township Jones recorded the names of those then in possession of each lot.

Today Barton Township has passed out of existence, its lands having been gobbled up by the urban sprawl of the city of Hamilton. But the orderly pattern of Jones' original survey still exists. The concession roads have become the main east-west arteries of the city: Burlington, Barton, Main, Concession, Fennell, Mohawk, Limeridge, Stone Church and Rymal. The side roads are the main north-south streets from Strathearn on the east to Paradise on the west.

In 1791 Quebec was divided into Lower Canada and Upper Canada. The first parliament of Upper Canada assembled at Niagara the following year under Lieutenant-Governor John Graves Simcoe. Simcoe wanted the capital of the province moved to an inland location. He chose a site on the Thames River. Jones was instructed to survey a route from the head of Cootes Paradise to the site. The Queen's Rangers cleared the route which is still known locally as Governor's Road. In Simcoe's plans, Cootes Paradise (Dundas) was to be a garrison town. But York, instead of London, became the capital and his plans for Cootes Paradise were developed no further.

Jones then surveyed two townships to the north of Governor's Road (Beverly and West Flamborough) and one to the south (Ancaster). Thus Jones had a hand in surveying all of the town-

KING'S HEAD INN
(Based on a sketch by Mrs. Simcoe)

John Ross Robertson Collection, Metropolitan Toronto Library Board

ships which later made up Wentworth County. From 1791 to 1816, however, the townships on the Flamborough side of the Governor's Road were part of York County in the Home District and the remaining ones were part of Lincoln County in the Niagara District.

In 1794 the King's Head Inn was built at government expense on the eastern end of the sand strip at the Head of the Lake for the accommodation of travellers in these parts. Simcoe also intended it as a military outpost for the planned garrison town of Cootes Paradise. It no doubt comforted him to know that the other end of the beach strip was guarded by Joseph Brant. Governor and Mrs. Simcoe stayed at the inn when they visited here in 1796. Mrs. Simcoe described it as having a "pretty plan." Augustus Jones served as its proprietor for a time.

Meanwhile, the settlers at the Head of the Lake continued the task of improving their farms. Jobs which were too big for one family to handle alone became the occasion for a "bee" to which the neighbours were invited. Many hands made light work of such tasks as clearing land, raising a new house or barn, pulling stumps or harvesting. Food and drink were provided by the host and a dance often ended the day. The women folk had their own bees. They got together to spin, to quilt, to preserve, and to exchange neighbourhood news. Bees also provided an opportunity for the young folks to get together. Their favourite was a corn-husking bee, for any lad finding a red ear among the yellow ones was permitted to kiss the young lady of his choice. Marriages amongst the pioneering families were soon taking place.

Governor Simcoe encouraged immigration to Canada from the United States. Offers of free, uncleared land were advertised. Partially cleared land could be purchased for a small sum. New settlers were attracted to Upper Canada by these opportunities. As this area became more settled, craftsmen came to ply their trades. Some travelled from house to house performing their services in return for meals and lodgings. Others set up shops.

The villages of Ancaster, Cootes Paradise, Stoney Creek and Wellington Square (Burlington) made their appearance. But there was nothing on the marshy plain between the escarpment and the south shore of Burlington Bay that might yet be called a village.

There were no ministers residing at the Head of the Lake for many years. Travelling missionaries made infrequent visits to administer the sacraments. But the people met on their own for prayer and worship. By 1801 the Methodists were meeting regularly under the leadership of Richard Springer. A Church of Scotland congregation was formed soon thereafter. By 1810 an Anglican congregation had erected a small frame church on Mohawk Road.

The ancient Indian trails were gradually improved. Where several of them met at today's intersection of King and Wellington Streets, a man by the name of Smith erected the district's first tavern. In Smith's tavern the first meeting of the Masonic Barton Lodge was held in 1795. Its charter members included Joseph Brant, Richard Beasley, Charles Depew and the sons of Robert Land. In 1806 a society known as the Burlington Board of Agriculture was formed to promote better agricultural practices in this area.

From endeavours such as these, community spirit gradually developed among the settlers at the Head of the Lake.

Bibliography

Part III (c. 1775-1810)

Beattie, Jessie L., *The Split in the Sky*, Toronto, Ryerson, 1960.

Burkholder, Mabel and Woodhouse, T. Roy, "Crown Patentees of Barton," *Wentworth Bygones*, I, (1958), pp. 34-36.

Campbell, Marjorie Freeman, *Niagara, Hinge of the Golden Arc*, Toronto, Ryerson, 1958, pp. 115-161.

Campbell, Patrick, *Travels in the Interior Inhabited Parts of North America, 1791-1792*, Toronto, The Champlain Society, 1937.

Cruikshank, E. A., "Petitions for Grants of Land," *Ontario Historical Society Papers and Records*, XXIV, (1927), pp. 26, 84.

Emery, Claire and Ford, Barbara, *From Pathway to Skyway, A History of Burlington*, Burlington, 1967, pp. 11-26.

Guillet, Edwin, *The Pioneer Farmer and Backwoodsman*, 2 vol., Toronto, Ontario Publishing Co., 1963.

Guillet, Edwin, *Pioneer Days in Upper Canada*, Toronto, University of Toronto Press, 1963.

Innis, Mary Quayle (ed.), *Mrs. Simcoe's Diary*, Toronto, Macmillan, 1965.

Laidler, George, "The Story of the Land Family," *Wentworth Bygones*, I, (1958), pp. 14-26.

Land, John H., "Record of Robert Land, U.E.L.," *Wentworth Historical Society Papers and Records*, VII, (1916), pp. 5-8.

Land, John H., "Odd Characters," *Wentworth Historical Society Papers and Records*, VIII, (1919), pp. 40-46.

La Rochefoucault Liancourt, Duke de, *Travels through the United States of North America, The Country of the Iroquois, and Upper Canada, in the Years 1795, 1796, and 1797*, 2 vol., London, Phillips, 1799.

Leblovic, Nicholas, "The Life and History of Richard Beasley, Esquire," *Wentworth Bygones*, VII, (1967), pp. 3-16.

McCullough, Charles R., "The Coming of the Loyalists," *The Hamilton Centennial, 1846-1946*, pp. 13-15.

Miller, Orlo, *Raiders of the Mohawk, The Story of Butler's Rangers*, Toronto, Macmillan, 1954.

Powell, R. Janet, "Choose One Knight with Sword," *Wentworth Bygones*, III, (1962), pp. 35-43.

Robertson, H. H., "The First Agricultural Society," *Wentworth Historical Society Papers and Records*, VII, (1916), pp. 11-12.

Stone, William, *Life of Joseph Brant (Thayendanegea)*, 2 vol., Albany, Munsell, 1865.

Trueman, A. W., *The Story of the United Empire Loyalists*, Toronto, Copp Clark, 1946.

Woodhouse, T. Roy, "A Year in the Life of an Ancaster Pioneer," *Wentworth Bygones*, VI, (1965), pp. 31-35.

Woodhouse, T. Roy, "The Beginnings of the History of Hamilton," *Wentworth Bygones*, V, (1964), pp. 23-27.

Part IV

. . . to the defence
of this province

1810	Brock made commander-in-chief of troops in Upper Canada
1812	war declared (June 18)
	Brock captures Detroit (Aug. 16)
	Battle of Queenston Heights (Oct. 13)
1813	Americans raid York (April 27)
	King's Head Inn burned (May 10)
	Americans turned back at Stoney Creek (June 6)
	British fleet defeated on Lake Erie (Sept. 10)
	Burlington Races (Sept. 28)
1814	Ancaster Assize (May, June)
	Battle of Lundy's Lane (July 25)
	Treaty of Ghent ends war (Dec. 24)

13

Every Male Inhabitant

Niagara, July the 2nd, 1812.

Dear Wife— . . . I have to request of you to send me three blankets, as I am destitute, and so are my brothers.

Angus McAfee
(Griffin, *W.H.S. Papers and Records*, IV, p. 113)

No one was more concerned about the defence of Upper Canada than Governor Simcoe. He personally drafted the militia act passed at the first parliament of Upper Canada in 1793. Every male inhabitant from the age of sixteen to fifty was required to enrol in the local militia company. A later amendment raised the age to sixty.

Every militia captain had to call out and inspect his company at least twice yearly. Failure to attend carried a fine of ten shillings for a private or non-commissioned officer and forty shillings for a commissioned officer. Several companies made up a regiment. The commanding officer of every regiment was required to muster it once a year on the fourth day of June (the king's birthday).

Inhabitants of the townships of Beverly and East and West Flamborough were members of the 2nd York Regiment. Richard Beasley became its commander in 1803. Most of its early officers were prominent Loyalists. The residents of the remaining townships which today made up Wentworth County became members of the 5th Lincoln Regiment. Its list of officers also included the names of many of the area's earliest settlers.

The men responded with varying attitudes when they were called out for inspection. Some settlers who had to travel many miles through undeveloped country considered it a great inconvenience. It was no doubt easier to pay the fine. Others regarded it as a pleasant outing—an opportunity to see their friends and enjoy the liquid refreshments which invariably followed. But for many, especially for those of Loyalist background, membership in

56

MILITIA TRAINING ON THE KING'S BIRTHDAY

the militia was a serious responsibility. They shared Simcoe's concern that it was only a question of time until the United States of America tried to extend its borders to include their part of the continent. Britain, deeply involved in European conflict, was able to provide only a token force for the defence of her overseas colony.

The militia, however, received very little real military training. Every man was required to furnish his own weapons. No uniforms were issued but those who still had theirs from the Revolutionary War were permitted to wear them.

When Isaac Brock became responsible for the defence of Upper Canada, he realized how essential but inadequate the militia was. He introduced changes to make it more effective. Two volunteer flank companies were raised from each regiment. These received regular training and were to be the first called for active service in the event of an emergency. Generally those who volunteered to serve in the flank companies were men known for their patriotism and willingness to fight. James Durand, William Davis, Peter Jones, John Land, James Gage, Nathaniel Hughson and John

Depew were a few of the names which appeared on the roll of the 2nd Flank Company of the 5th Lincoln Militia when it was first established.

When the long-anticipated war with the United States came in June, 1812, the flank companies were immediately called out. Those of the 5th Lincoln Regiment reached the Niagara frontier within a few days of the declaration of war.

In a letter from Fort George to a superior on July 12, Brock had high praise for the militia:

The militia, which assembled here immediately on the account being received of war being declared by the United States, have been improving daily in discipline. . . .

The alacrity and good temper with which the militia, in the first instance, marched to the frontiers, have tended to infuse in the mind of the enemy a very different sentiment of the disposition of the inhabitants, who, he was led to believe would, upon the first summons, declare themselves an American state.

(Tupper, pp. 202-203)

Brock's concern for the militia, however, was evident:

Nearly the whole of the arms at my disposal have been issued. They are barely sufficient to arm the militia immediately required to guard the frontier . . . . The militia assembled in a wretched state in regard to clothing; many were without shoes, an article which can scarcely be provided in the country.

(Tupper, p. 203)

For the most part, the militiamen were used for routine war-time duties, thus freeing the highly-trained British regulars for the actual fighting. Militiamen found themselves guarding lines of communication, doing garrison duty, escorting prisoners of war, rounding up those who failed to report for duty and foraging for supplies and rations. They knew the country and were used to good effect against enemy patrols and foraging parties.

But militiamen were also present at every fighting engagement that took place in Upper Canada. A special company made up of men from the Head of the Lake and known as Captain Hatt's Company of Volunteers joined with militiamen from other parts of the province in Brock's enterprise against Detroit. One flank company from the 5th Lincoln Regiment and three flank companies of the York Militia were present at the Battle of Queenston Heights. Local militiamen did their part to hasten the retreat of the Americans from Stoney Creek.

In 1813 the Volunteer Incorporated Militia Battalion was raised by voluntary enlistment from the militia units. Several local residents served in this special corps for the duration of the war. The battalion bore the brunt of the action for a considerable time at the Battle of Lundy's Lane and received special commendation for its part in it.

The militia has been criticized for its high desertion rate during the war. But is it not understandable that many risked severe penalty to make a visit to their families to ensure that all was well or to assist with the planting and harvesting? Militiamen could not fight with the detachment of professional soldiers. Their only objective was to rid the country of the enemy as quickly as possible so they could return in peace to their homes.

14

The Battle of Stoney Creek

Burlington Heights,
Sunday, 6th June, 1813.

Information has just been received that the Enemy has entirely aban-doned his Camp, burnt his Tents, destroyed his Provisions, ammuni-tion, etc., and retired precipitately towards the 40 Mile Creek.

Colonel John Harvey
(*W.H.S. Papers and Records*, II, p. 98-99)

After the setbacks they suffered at Detroit and Queenston in 1812, the Americans were determined to reverse their fortunes of war in 1813. A massive three-pronged attack was planned: from Detroit into the western part of Upper Canada; across the Niagara frontier; and against the St. Lawrence region by way of Lake Champlain.

On May 27, the long-anticipated offensive across the Niagara River against Fort George was launched. After three hours of intensive fighting, the British under General Vincent were forced to abandon the fort to the Americans. The British forces retreated to Beaver Dams by nightfall. There they were joined by the garri-sons from Fort Erie and Chippawa. Vincent dismissed the militia. Many, certain that Vincent was withdrawing from the Niagara peninsula thus leaving it prey to the advancing Americans, anxiously returned to their homes. A few remained with the retreating British army.

Falling back through the peninsula, Vincent reached Burling-ton Heights on the evening of May 31. With him were some 1700 soldiers: a detachment of the Royal Artillery, the 8th (King's), 41st, 49th and Royal Newfoundland Regiments, the Glengarry Light Infantry and a squad of dragoons. Vincent had two alterna-tives. He could continue his retreat to Kingston or he could dig in for a stand at the heights. If he abandoned the heights, it would leave a corridor into the central part of the province open to the Americans. Vincent, after consultation with his officers, decided to face the enemy. The soldiers and militiamen were set to work constructing log barricades and earthworks across the high ground which was flanked on one side by the bay and on the other by the marsh.

Meanwhile, the Americans had planned to cross the lake by boat and cut off Vincent's retreat. But high winds and heavy seas kept them from getting started. A land pursuit was organized and on the afternoon of June 5 a force of some 3,000 men neared the Head of the Lake.

An American advance patrol skirmished briefly with a British outpost in the vicinity of Big (Red Hill) Creek. The American patrol returned to the main body and camp was set up for the night on the farm of James Gage. Plans were made to meet the enemy, which was encamped less than eight miles away, on the morrow.

When news of the Americans' approach was carried to the British camp, Colonel Harvey, second in command to Vincent, went out with a small patrol to reconnoitre. William Merritt, a militia officer and an eyewitness, described the American position:

The enemy were camped on Gage's fields, in a very advantageous position; 2,000 of their men were on the hill to the right of the road, and 500 in a lane on the left, in advance of their artillery, which was situated on a hill directly in front of the road that our troops must come. . . .   (Merritt, p. 24)

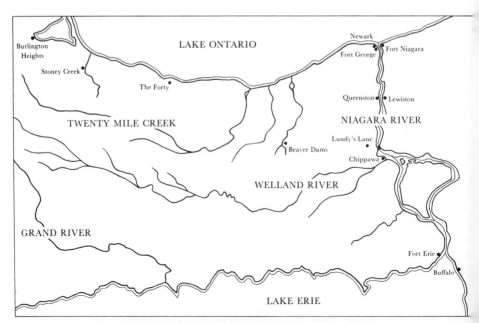

THE NIAGARA PENINSULA—WAR OF 1812

EARTHWORKS, HAMILTON CEMETERY

These were constructed across Burlington Heights by the British army in 1813.

WAR OF 1812 CANNON (9-POUNDER)
Similar guns, mounted on large wooden wheels, were used by the Americans at the Battle of Stoney Creek.

From the information gathered, Harvey convinced Vincent of the wisdom of a surprise night attack. It might serve to throw the Americans off balance or it would at least serve as a cover for a British retreat from the heights. Vincent placed Harvey in charge. From the 8th Regiment commanded by Major Ogilvie and the 49th Regiment under Major Plenderleath, 704 professional soldiers were selected. The others remained as a reserve force at the heights.

Shortly before midnight the attackers set out down the dark trails that are now York Street and King Street. They carried only their guns and ammunition. The order was for absolute silence. Guns were unloaded lest one should be accidentally fired. Past William Davis' log tavern at Big Creek they stole.

The enemy sentries were encountered and silently subdued; the outpost in the Methodist church about half a mile west of the main camp was captured. Into the flat before the enemy camp stormed the British—Harvey and Lieutenant James Fitzgibbon in the centre, Plenderleath to the left and Ogilvie to the right. Here is Colonel Harvey's official account of the action which followed:

The surprise was tolerably complete; but our Troops incautiously advancing and charging across the line of the Camp fires, and a few musquets being fired (notwithstanding my exertions to check it), our line was distinctly seen by the Enemy, whose Troops in some degree recovered from the Panick, and formed upon the

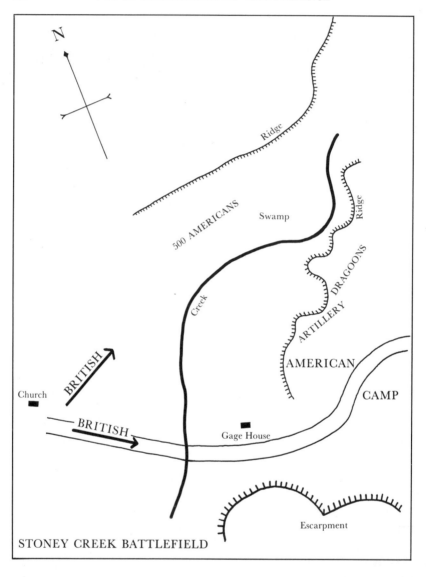

STONEY CREEK BATTLEFIELD

surrounding heights, poured a destructive fire of musquetry upon us, which was answered on our part by repeated charges whenever a body of the Enemy could be discovered or reached. The King's regiment and part of the 49th charged and carried the 4 Field pieces in very gallant style, and the whole sustained with un-daunted firmness the heavy fire which was occasionally poured upon them.   (*W.H.S. Papers and Records*, II, p. 98)

In less than three-quarters of an hour, the Americans had been routed. Several field guns and about 100 prisoners, including the two American generals, Chandler and Winder, were captured by the British. But the British paid dearly for their success with 23 killed, 136 wounded and 55 missing. The British withdrew from the field before daybreak lest the Americans discover their small numbers and rally for a counterattack.

The Americans did return to the scene but only to destroy what they could not carry off. Their eastward retreat was hastened by the Indian war cries of the militia which hung on their flanks and rear. They were further harassed, upon halting at Forty Mile Creek, by the British fleet lying offshore. The Americans decided to abandon the offensive and retired to Fort George.

Although it was not immediately realized, it was on that eventful night at Stoney Creek that the tide of war in Upper Canada was turned in Britain's favour.

BATTLE OF STONEY CREEK, 1813
The artist shows the British troops charging the American artillery.

C. W. Jefferys, Imperial Oil Collection

15

Scout Billy Green

Fort George, 8th June, 1813.

From the Forty Mile Creek we learn that the affair at Stoney Creek was very serious. The confusion was great. Some spy or deserter procured the countersign at our encampment, went to the British camp and in 5 minutes after he entered General Vincent's tent the English army was in motion. Our camp was entered without opposition by means of the above mentioned treachery. . . .

From a letter to the editors of the Baltimore *Whig*
(Cruikshank, *Documentary History*, vi, p. 46-47)

The tradition has long been cherished that a decisive role in the outcome of the battle at Stoney Creek was played by one of the local lads, young Billy Green. One searches the official military reports of the battle in vain for some reference to him. British generals and colonels did not include such details in their reports to their superiors. But Green's own account of that eventful night, as told in later years to his grandson and recorded by him, has survived.

Motherless since infancy, Billy was the son of Adam Green, a Saltfleet settler. Billy, schooled in the forests that surrounded his home, became a skilled and adventurous woodsman.

On the morning of June 5, 1813, 19-year-old Billy and Levi, his brother, followed the escarpment eastward to the Forty (Grimsby) where they watched for the advancing Americans. When the latter reached the Forty, Billy claimed:

We stayed there until all the enemy but a few had passed through the village. Then we yelled like Indians. I tell you, those simple fellows did run.

(*Hamilton Spectator*, March 12, 1938)

Billy and his brother then sped back to their home near Stoney Creek. Billy, unable to remain idle for long, decided to go down to the lakeshore to visit his brother-in-law, Isaac Corman, and find out how he and his family were faring. Here is Billy's account of what followed:

When I got there I whistled, and out came Keziah, my sister (Corman's wife). I asked her where Isaac was, and she said the enemy had taken him prisoner and taken the trail to the beach. . . . I started and ran; every now and then I would whistle until I got across the creek. When I heard Isaac's hoot like an owl I thought the enemy had him there, but he was coming back alone. I was going to raise an Indian warwhoop and scare them when I saw Isaac coming. I asked how he got away, and he said: "The major and I got a-talking, and he said he was second cousin to General Harrison. I said I was a first cousin to General Harrison, and came from Kentucky. After talking a little longer a message came for the major; he said, 'I must go; you may go home, Corman.' I said I couldn't get through the lines. 'I will give you the countersign,' and he did." Isaac gave the countersign to me; I got it and away I came.

Billy then borrowed Levi's old horse and headed along the top of the escarpment around the Big Creek (Albion) ravine. He continued on foot to Burlington Heights where the British forces were camped. His tale continued:

When I got there they took me for a spy, and I had to tell them all I knew before they would believe me. It was about 11 o'clock P.M. I explained to Colonel Harvey where and how the American army were encamped near Stoney Creek. He suggested a night attack on the enemy. After Colonel Harvey had a short interview with General Vincent, it was decided to start at once for Stoney Creek, and they commenced to hustle.

We got started about 11:30 P.M. Colonel Harvey asked me if I knew the way, and I said, "Yes, every inch of it." He gave me a corporal's sword and told me to take the lead. Sometimes I would get away ahead and go back to hurry them up. I told them it would be daylight before we got there if we did not hurry. Some one said that would be soon enough to be killed.

. . . I espied a sentry leaning against a tree. I told the man behind to shoot him, but Colonel Harvey said, "No, run him through," and he was dispatched. The next sentry was at the church. He discharged his gun and demanded a pass. I grabbed his gun with one hand and put my sword to him with the other.

His narrative concluded with a description of the actual battle, essentially as it was recorded in the official military accounts.

Thus in the years since 1813, most local residents have believed, without a shadow of a doubt, that it was their own Billy Green who was responsible for the success of the surprise night attack. And, when the monument commemorating the 100th anniversary of the battle was erected, Billy's part in it was recognized. Around the monument are eight shields, each bearing the name of a hero of that important engagement. Scout Green's name appears on one of them.

STONEY CREEK MONUMENT
This tower was erected in 1913 to commemorate the 100th anniversary of the Battle of Stoney Creek.

BILLY GREEN'S SWORD
Philip Green displays the sword given to his great-great-grandfather on the night of the battle.

Hamilton Spectator

16

On the Home Front

After the battle was over we got William Gage's oxen and stoneboat and his son Peter, John Lee, John Yeager, I and several others buried the dead soldiers on a knoll near the road where the enemy placed their guns. . . .

Billy Green
(*Hamilton Spectator*, March 12, 1938)

Many have been the times that families at the Head of the Lake have watched their menfolk depart for battle in other parts of Canada or in distant lands. But at no time has war so closely touched the lives of those left behind as it did during the War of 1812. Deeds of courage and sacrifice occurred not just on the battlefields. Those remaining on the home front at the Head of the Lake also did their part to repel the Americans' advance.

After the hustle and bustle of seeing fathers and elder sons off to war, the women and younger children turned to the running of the farm. In addition to fulfilling their own needs, they were required to furnish food and livestock for the troops. Foraging parties roamed this area searching for provisions for the military depot at Burlington Heights. An order signed by General Vincent read:

You are hereby authorized to put in requisition for the account of the army, all such cattle as you shall be able to discover, using the quickest means, and selecting such as may belong to persons having the greatest resources; in other respects, you will, as far as may be practicable, allow to each family a milch cow, and to every farmer one working team . . . .

(Griffin, *W.H.S. Papers and Records*, IV, p. 114)

Payment was supposed to be made for these provisions but in the confusion of war, this was often not done.

As the American forces advanced through the peninsula after the fall of Fort George, enemy foraging parties also scoured the countryside. Many settlers drove their animals into the shelter of the forests and hid their family treasures. Mary Land, on learning of the Americans' approach, buried the family valuables and the jewels belonging to the Barton Lodge under a large peony bush in her garden. Many in the peninsula evacuated their homes only to find them, upon their return, pillaged and sometimes destroyed.

In May, 1813, a drama involving another of the local women allegedly took place. Two American schooners were sent to the western lakehead to destroy the King's Head Inn and the military supplies stored there. The superior invading force was more than a match for Major Sam Hatt and the men of the local militia who had been assigned to guard the inn. They withdrew from the scene to await reinforcements. Meanwhile, the inn was destroyed and its stores were removed to the American ships.

According to family tradition, Mrs. Bates, the daughter-in-law of the proprietor, was so angered at the destruction of her home and possessions that she rowed out to the ships and insisted on the return of those things that had been taken and payment for what had been destroyed. Such was her ire that not only did the captain grant her demands, but gallantly ordered some of his crew to row her ashore!

On the evening of June 5, 1813, when the American forces reached Stoney Creek, Billy Green said that they refreshed themselves and their horses at the expense of John Brady, the owner of a tavern there, "and did not leave his premises until they had eaten and drunk all they could find around his place." When the Americans camped on the James Gage farm, the Gage family was locked in the cellar. The American officers made the rest of the house their headquarters. Neighbours were likewise seized and held captive lest they warn the British. Fence rails became fuel for campfires. During the battle, the nearby Methodist church, one of the earliest in these parts, was riddled with musket shot and damaged by cannon fire.

The morning after the engagement, the local inhabitants flocked to view the scene. The battleground was strewn with men and equipment. The task of burying the dead and tending the wounded fell to the local residents. Homes in the area became hospitals. Women became nurses. Dr. William Case, the area's pioneer doctor, worked side by side with the military surgeons.

Modern medical practices were unknown. Recovery was more a matter of good fortune than of skill on the part of the doctors. When Mrs. Titus G. Simons of West Flamborough received word that her husband had been severely wounded at the battle of Lundy's Lane, she immediately "mounted her horse, took her infant in her arms, and followed by one attendant, rode with speed to her husband's side."

Robertson, W.H.S. Papers and Records, II, p. 53

How much her being at his side hastened his recovery one does not know but he recuperated and later became the sheriff of this district.

Every family then living in these parts had its own stories to tell about the war. A study of family records and conversations with their descendants rewards the searcher with a considerable collection of anecdotes which are sometimes touching, sometimes amusing, sometimes doubtful, but seldom dull.

GAGE HOUSE ON STONEY CREEK BATTLEFIELD
James Gage and his family were imprisoned in the cellar by the Americans who made the house their headquarters on June 5, 1813. It is now a museum.

17

The Burlington Races

Behind them was the American fleet in pursuit, ahead of them the white breakers lashing on the beach. There was not a moment to lose. If the smaller British vessels could get through the cut, it was certain that the Americans, with larger, clumsier vessels and more imperfect knowledge of the coast, could not.

Hamilton Spectator, July 15, 1936

Had any of the residents at the Head of the Lake been gazing out over Lake Ontario on September 28, 1813, it is unlikely that they would have observed the drama taking place there. For the day which was quickly waning was stormy and visibility was poor.

Looking toward Burlington Bay the next morning, however, the local inhabitants would have been amazed to see large war ships riding on its waters. How did they get there? The only entrance through the sand strip into the bay was a small natural channel which was much too shallow, everyone thought, for ships of that size to navigate.

To most of the inhabitants of Upper Canada, especially those living in the Niagara Peninsula, the War of 1812 was a land war, a war of marching feet and rattling musket fire. But military experts of the day knew that naval control of the Great Lakes' waterways was essential to the defence of Upper Canada.

Commander of the small British naval fleet on Lake Ontario was Sir James Yeo. His duties were twofold. The first was to prevent his American counterpart, Commodore Isaac Chauncey, with his larger and stronger fleet, from gaining control of the lake. The second was to safeguard the movement of supplies and troops. The clumsy, top-heavy sailing vessels of the two fleets played tag up and down the lake throughout the summer of 1813.

On the morning of September 23, Yeo's fleet of two ships, two brigs and two schooners dropped anchor off York. They had just completed an uneventful run to the Head of the Lake with a load of supplies for the military camp there.

Shortly before noon, the sails of Chauncey's superior fleet (two ships, three brigs and six schooners) appeared on the horizon to the east of York. All were heavily armed. Although Chauncey unquestionably had the advantage, Yeo decided to engage the American fleet in battle. It was not in the tradition of the British navy to flee before the enemy. Moreover, it might divert Chauncey from another raid against York like the one he had carried out in July.

From his flagship *Wolfe,* Yeo directed the attack against the centre of the approaching line of American vessels. The distance between the two fleets shortened. Flagship engaged flagship at close range and both were severely damaged. Slowly the smaller American vessels, aided by a rising easterly wind, were manoeuvring into position to join the fight.

Yeo broke off the action and headed for shelter at the Head of

C. W. Jefferys, Imperial Oil Collection

NAVAL ACTION ON LAKE ONTARIO, 1813

the Lake. Chauncey followed, certain that he could overtake the crippled British fleet or box it in at the end of the lake.

Through a rising storm the chase was run. But as Chauncey approached the end of the lake, he was puzzled. The British fleet gave no hint of turning. Chauncey dared not go closer lest his awkward vessels become caught in the wind and current and pile up in the pounding surf. Confident that this was the fate of the British vessels, he turned towards Niagara.

But Yeo had a bold plan. He summoned his pilot, James Richard, a twenty-two-year-old Canadian lad, who knew every shoal and channel in the lake. They conversed and decided to try to run the narrow channel into Burlington Bay. The easterly wind which had grown to gale force had raised the water level at the western lakehead. With the wind behind them, there just might be enough water in the channel. The schooners and brigs went in without difficulty. The crews of the other ships watched with bated breath as Yeo's flagship made its attempt. With her keel scraping bottom, she rode in on the crest of the waves!

The British fleet waited out the storm in the sheltered waters of the bay. Repairs to the damaged ships were made under the protection of the gun batteries on Burlington Heights. Then began the difficult task of getting the ships back through the channel. The smaller vessels went first. As much equipment as possible was removed from the larger vessels. Their anchors were then hauled out into the lake and, their crews straining at the capstans, the vessels were inched back through the channel. Yeo, with his fleet intact, set sail for Kingston.

Chauncey, confident that only the battered hulls of the British vessels rested on the sands at the Head of the Lake, had already set sail for his base at Sackett's Harbour. How puzzled he must have been to learn later that the British fleet was safe in Kington harbour!

18

"The Bloody Assize"

I earlier saw eight men hanged on the other side of Locke street near Dundurn. . . . There was a rude gallows with eight nooses. Four victims stood in each of two wagons which had been drawn under the gallows. They stood on boards laid across the wagons while the hangman adjusted the nooses, then the wagons were driven off.

John Ryckman
(Woodhouse, *Wentworth Bygones*, v, p. 25)

Before the shadow of war lifted from the Head of the Lake, one more event took place there—an event which further engraved the grim reality of war on the minds and emotions of the local inhabitants.

The Americans had expected little opposition when they declared war and planned their invasion of Upper Canada. Were not the majority of inhabitants former residents of the United States? Many were not Loyalists. They were more recent immigrants who had been lured by offers of free or cheap land. The Americans were certain that these settlers were dissatisfied with British rule and would welcome the chance to live again under the American flag.

How wrong they were! Most of the latecomers stood shoulder to shoulder with their Loyalist neighbours to repel the invaders. However, some did sympathize with the American cause and gave it their moral support. A few even aided the enemy actively. They crossed the border to join the American forces or acted as spies and raiders for them.

Andrew Markle was one of a group that shortly before the war had purchased the mill once owned by Beasley at Ancaster. When war broke out, Markle became the leader of a gang engaged in pro-American activities in the Chatham area. A small detachment of militia was sent to apprehend the gang. Only Markle and one other escaped.

73

Those who were captured, along with several others, were imprisoned at York while preparations were made to bring them to trial. The authorities felt that they must deal harshly with them to discourage others from engaging in similar activities. A suitable place for the trials was sought. The choice finally settled on the bustling community of Ancaster. The military camp on Burlington Heights was close by to furnish supplies and guards. The Union Hotel, then in use as a military hospital, was cleared for use as the court house.

THE UNION HOTEL, ANCASTER
The trials of those charged with treason during the War of 1812 were held in this building which is still standing (1969).

The court convened in the latter part of May, 1814. Prosecutor for the Crown was the young acting attorney-general, John Beverley Robinson. His role at the trials was the beginning of a long career of public service to his province. Three judges of the Court of King's Bench took turns in presiding. The charge against the men was high treason. Each awaited his turn to appear before judge and jury. Ironically, according to local tradition, the accused were held in the nearby stone mill, the mill of which Andrew Markle was part owner.

The trials continued for two weeks. Of the nineteen tried, one pleaded guilty, fourteen were convicted on evidence and four were acquitted. On June 21 the presiding judge donned the black hood to pass sentence on those found guilty. The wording of the sentence for high treason had remained unchanged from medieval times; each was to be "hanged"' by the neck but not until his Death for he must be cut down alive and his Entrails taken out and burned before his Face, his Head then to be cut off and his Body divided into four Quarters and His Head and Quarters to be at the King's Disposal."

Execution normally took place "the next day but one" after sentencing but it was delayed for a month to give the condemned men an opportunity to plead for mercy. Appeals on their behalf from wives, relatives, friends and prominent citizens poured in. After careful consideration by the Executive Council of Upper Canada, seven were granted reprieves. They were taken to the Kingston jail to await "His Majesty's pleasure." One escaped on the way. Three died the following winter from jail fever (typhus). The property of those remaining was confiscated and they were banished for life from British territory.

For the other eight, however, there were no reprieves and on July 20 they were taken to the gallows erected just outside the military camp on Burlington Heights. The sheriff of the Niagara district was assigned to carry out the execution.

It is not recorded how many of the local inhabitants witnessed the grim spectacle that took place that day. But hangings were public events in those times and large crowds usually gathered to watch them. Moreover, the authorities wished for the execution of these men to serve as an example to the rest of the population. Therefore, many were likely on hand to view the carrying out of the mediaeval sentence on the eight men. But the execution was never conducted as pronounced. The hangman did the job and the bodies were not cut down until after death had occurred.

The trial and execution climaxed the war for the inhabitants at the Head of the Lake. Once again they turned to peaceful pursuits as farmers, merchants and craftsmen. Never since have enemy soldiers trod the ground at the Head of the Lake. Never since has the shadow of war hung so heavily over its inhabitants. But a deep-rooted distrust of American ideas and ambitions remained in the minds of the citizens of Upper Canada for several decades.

Bibliography

Part IV (War of 1812)

Ballantyne, Lareine, *The Scout Who Led an Army*, Toronto, Macmillan, 1963.

Biggar, E. B., "Sketch of the Battle of Stoney Creek," *Hamilton Spectator*, June 7 & 9, 1873.

Corman, Hazel A., "An Account of the Battle of Stoney Creek," *Wentworth Historical Society Papers and Records*, VII, (1916), pp. 26-34.

Cruikshank, E. A. (ed.), *The Documentary History of the Campaign on the Niagara Frontier*, Vol. VI, Welland, Lundy's Lane Historical Society.

Cruikshank, E. A., "John Beverley Robinson and the Trials for Treason in 1814," *Ontario Historical Society Papers and Records*, XXV, (1929), pp. 191-219.

Cruikshank, E. A., "The Battle of Stoney Creek," *Wentworth Bygones*, IV, (1963), pp. 1-8.

Griffin, Justus A. (ed.), "Militia Rolls of 1812," *Wentworth Historical Society Papers and Records*, IV, (1905), pp. 109-115.

Hamilton Spectator, "British Vessels Elude Enemy Near Hamilton," July 15, 1936.

Hamilton Spectator, "Descendants of Billy the Scout Recall His Deeds," March 12, 1938, p. 21.

Hamilton Spectator, special edition—150th anniversary of the Battle of Stoney Creek, June 6, 1963.

Johnston, Charles M., and others, *A Battle for the Heartland*, Stoney Creek, Pennell, 1963.

Jones, Frank L., "The Burlington Races," *Wentworth Bygones*, V, (1964), pp. 18-22.

Jones, Frank L., "The Militia of Upper Canada: The Formative Years," *Wentworth Bygones*, VI, (1965), pp. 1-13.

Land, J. H., "The Battle of Stoney Creek," *Wentworth Historical Society Papers and Records*, I, (1892), pp. 21-27.

Merritt, J. P., *Biography of the Hon. W. H. Merritt, M.P.*, St. Catharines, Leavenworth, 1875, pp. 22-25.

Provincial Statutes of Upper Canada, Revised, Collected and Republished by Authority, York, R. C. Horne, 1818, pp. 222-225.

Riddell, W. R., "An Echo of the War of 1812," *Ontario Historical Society Papers and Records*, XXIII, (1926), pp. 434-449.

Riddell, W. R., "The Ancaster 'Bloody Assize' of 1814," *The Defended Border*, Morris Zaslow (ed.), Toronto, Macmillan, 1964, pp. 241-250.

Robertson, H. H., "Major Titus Gear Simons at Lundy's Lane," *Wentworth Historical Society Papers and Records*, II, (1899), pp. 49-54.

Robertson, H. H., "Gore District Militia, and the Militia of West Lincoln and West York," *Wentworth Historical Society Papers and Records*, IV, (1905), pp. 9-64.

Robertson, H. H., "Lincoln Militia, 1812-14," *Wentworth Historical Society Papers and Records*, VIII, (1919), pp. 37-40.

Thompson, Mabel W., "Billy Green 'The Scout'," *Ontario History*, XLIV, (October, 1952), pp. 173-181.

Tupper, Ferdinand Brock (ed.), *The Life and Correspondence of Major-General Sir Isaac Brock*, London, 1847.

Wentworth Historical Society, "Documents Relating to the Battle of Stoney Creek," *Papers and Records*, II, (1899), pp. 94-103.

Wood, Herbert Fairlie, "The Many Battles of Stoney Creek," *Canadian Geographical Journal*, LXIV, (March, 1962), pp. 108-112.

Part V

. . . a fine town

1813?	George Hamilton's farm subdivided into lots
c. 1814	Wm. Sheldon opens first local store—corner of King and John Streets
1816	*population (Barton Township) 668*
	creation of District of Gore; Hamilton chosen district town
1818	log court house and jail
1821	Gore District School
1824	first local post office
	First Methodist Church—King Street East
1826	*population (Barton Township) 1,195*
	Burlington Canal opened
1828	stone court house
1829	first Hamilton newspaper, the *Gore Balance*
1832	cholera epidemic; great fire
1833	elected Board of Police; first municipal taxes
	local stage service between Hamilton and Dundas
1835	first fire engine
1836	*population (Hamilton) 2,846*
	Gore Bank
1837	MacNab knighted
1839	Mechanics' Institute founded
	Christ's Church—James Street North
	James Street market site
1842	street lamps (fish oil and camphine) at main intersections
1843	Hamilton - Port Dover plank road
1844	John Street South macadamized

19

The Birth of Hamilton

And be it further enacted by the authority aforesaid, That a Gaol and Court-House for the said District of Gore, shall be erected and built in some fit and convenient place, on Lot number fourteen, in the third concession of the Township of Barton, to be called the Town of Hamilton. . . .

Provincial Statutes of Upper Canada,
March 22, 1816

By 1810 the population at the Head of the Lake had shown considerable increase and settlers were finding it most inconvenient to have to travel to York or Niagara whenever they had to conduct any official business. They petitioned the government to create a new district at the lakehead from a portion of the Home District and a portion of the Niagara District.

Every community then in existence in this area had hopes of becoming the district town, the site of the court house and administrative offices for the newly created district. Ancaster, on the trail to the Grand River and the site of the first mill in these parts, was already a flourishing community. Its closest rival was Cootes Paradise (Dundas) laid out by Governor Simcoe at the eastern end of his road to the Thames. Located on a fine mill stream and a navigable waterway, it was destined to become an important centre. The residents of Brant's Block (Burlington) felt that their community should be the site chosen.

How the residents of those centres must have laughed when James Durand petitioned the government to make his farm the proposed town site! Durand had recently purchased the Daniel Springer grant, the property extending from today's James Street to Mary Street and from Main Street to the mountain-top. A later purchase from Nathaniel Hughson extended the property northward to King Street. The only residence on the property was a stone house built by Durand.

The part of Barton Township lying below the mountain was then only a series of half-cultivated farms. Had anyone foreseen a district town on the sloping plain between the bay front and the escarpment, he would likely have predicted its centre to be at the corner of today's King and Wellington Streets where the trails from Niagara, York and Brant's Ford met.

But Durand was serious and collected the signatures of over 200 local residents on his petition. The site of Cootes Paradise he ridiculed as being "at the head of a long frog marsh which is navigable only at particular seasons of the year." However, argument and speculation were interrupted by the War of 1812 and the plans to create the new district were set aside.

Meanwhile Durand moved to the Belleville area to engage in the manufacture of salt. He sold his property in Barton Township to George Hamilton. Hamilton was the son of Robert Hamilton of Queenston, a wealthy and influential wholesale merchant. The move of George and his family to the Head of the Lake was later described by a granddaughter:

When the war of 1812 with the United States broke out, George Hamilton was living at Niagara-on-the-Lake with his wife . . . and deeming the frontier town an unsafe place of residence, they journeyed on to Hamilton; the young mother with her baby boy, Robert Jarvis Hamilton, in her arms, riding on horseback through the bridlepaths till they reached their haven of refuge on the mountainside, above the beautiful waters of Burlington bay. . . .

(Lemon, *W.H.S. Papers and Records*, II, p. 136)

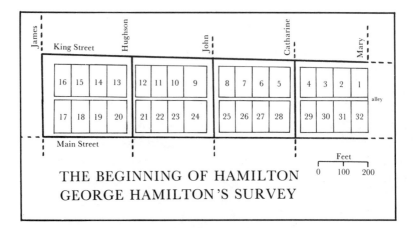

THE BEGINNING OF HAMILTON
GEORGE HAMILTON'S SURVEY

Hamilton had the northern portion of his farm surveyed and subdivided into four blocks of town lots, 16 of them fronting on present-day King Street and 16 on Main Street. According to tradition, this is supposed to have been done in 1813 but it seems unlikely that he would have had it done during the confusion of the war in which he took an active part. However, by 1816 several of the lots had been sold for residential and commercial purposes and the nucleus of a community had been established.

In the meantime, the government had dusted off the pre-war

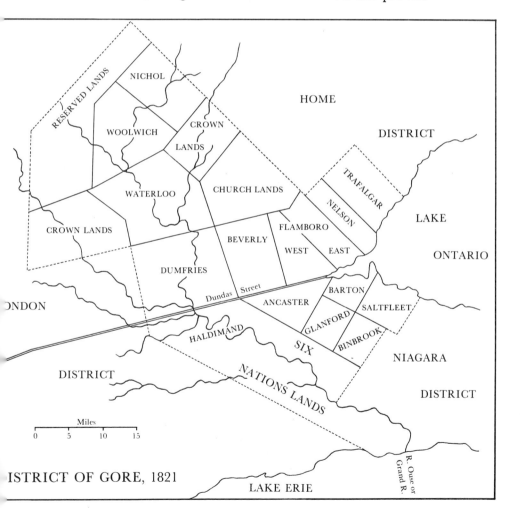

ISTRICT OF GORE, 1821

petitions and on March 22, 1816, the long-awaited bill to create a new district at the Head of the Lake was passed. It was to be known as the District of Gore and it was made up of the County of Wentworth and the County of Halton, both of which then covered a greater area than they do today.

BARTON TOWNSHIP, 1817

Inhabited Houses	130
Number of People	800
Churches or Places of Worship	1
Medical Practitioners	0
Schools	5
Stores	5
Taverns	4
Grist Mills	1
Saw Mills	4

SOURCE: Robert Gourlay, *Statistical Account of Upper Canada*, Vol. I, p. 402.

The act specified that the district town was to be situated on the property owned by Hamilton. It also indicated that the town was to bear Hamilton's name. This was a great source of annoyance to the residents of Ancaster and Dundas. For years they tried without success to have the location changed.

George Hamilton donated a two-block site for the erection of a combined court house and jail. It was described by one who remembered it:

The lower part, for criminals, was constructed four logs thick, and the second story, set apart for debtors, was made of three logs, and the third story, used as a court house, two logs thick.

(McKenzie, *W.H.S. Papers and Records*, I, p. 180)

It stood on the east side of John Street, across from the present court house. The first court sessions were held in it in 1818. To the south of today's court house Hamilton later donated a piece of property for public use as a market site.

He also donated the triangular piece of land now known as Gore Park as a "promenade" with the stipulation that it was never to be used for any other purpose. It was thought that

Nathaniel Hughson would give a complimentary piece of land on the north to complete a rectangular "town square" but this was never done.

Gradually the town of Hamilton blossomed and expanded beyond the original four-block limits. Many of the nearby streets including John, James, Catharine, Augusta and Hunter were named after members of Hamilton's family. Hamilton's service and benevolence on behalf of the fledgling community extended over almost a quarter century, and when he died in 1836 Hamiltonians sincerely mourned the passing of a beloved and respected leading citizen.

20

Education for Some of the Children

The day was bright and fair; 'twas June; the birds were loud in their songs, the trees fresh in their budding. We started for school in the early day with our lunch-baskets and books. On the way, says Harry, "Charlie, we will play truant to-day—go into the thick woods on a beautiful hill; sit down under a big tree . . . ."

Charles Durand, c. 1817
(*Reminiscences*, p. 29)

The settlers before 1800 were too busy getting established in a new land to give much attention to the provision of schools for their children. Sons, working side by side with their fathers, learned the arts of husbandry while daughters learned the skills

of homemaking from their mothers. In the evenings by the flickering light from the fireplace, some taught their children to read,
using what books they had. In many homes this was only the
Bible.

As communities became established, private schools made their
appearance. The first in these parts was at Ancaster in 1796. Even
at their best, such schools offered only a rudimentary education
and most of them closed their doors after only a few months. Few
settlers could afford the fees and the travelling distance was
usually too great for their children.

Those of wealth and position sometimes hired a tutor to
instruct their children at home. Some sent their children abroad.
George Hamilton, for example, was educated in "Edinbro'
Town." However, they avoided sending their children to schools
in the United States where their heads might become filled with
"republican ideas."

To the people of this so-called upper class, the education of
their children was of vital importance. One day their sons would
take their place as leaders of society in the professions and in the
government of the province. The fathers therefore felt that it
was the duty of the government to provide schools for their children. Education for the masses of children, however, they regarded as most unnecessary.

An act was passed in 1807 authorizing the establishment of a
school in each of the eight districts then in existence in Upper
Canada. Although supported by an annual grant from public
funds, attendance at these district schools was very much restricted
to a small minority of the children.

A district school in Hamilton was authorized following the
establishment of the Gore District in 1816. It opened its doors
in 1821 at the southwest corner of Hughson and Jackson Streets.
John Law was its first master.

Only boys were admitted, girls continuing to be educated at
home or in private schools. Both elementary and secondary education were given. Boys in the first class were taught reading and
spelling. "Tables" were introduced in the second class. By the
time a scholar reached the fifth class, he was receiving instruction

RUTHVEN's
BOOK-STORE PRINTING OFFICE, &
BINDERY,
HAMILTON, U. C.

JUST PUBLISHED,
AND FOR SALE AT THIS OFFICE,
WHOLESALE AND RETAIL,

Mayor's English Spelling Book,
Murray's 1st. Book for Children,
Do.   English Spelling Book,
Do.   Abridged Grammar,
Do.   Introduction to English Reader,
Do.   English Reader.
Primers, Toy Books, &c.
A variety of School Books, Stationary,
Slates, Ink, Plain and Ruled Copy Books,
&c., constantly kept and sold *cheap.*

BOOKBINDING,
Done in all its various branches by professed workmen.
Account Books, Ruled and bound to order with plain
and Spring back, on the shortest notice.
Merchants, Schoolmasters & Pedlars, will find it to
their advantage to deal at this Establishment.

LOCAL ADVERTISEMENT, 1840

in reading, spelling, arithmetic, grammar, geography, history, Latin, Greek and advanced mathematics. Most of the textbooks were from Britain. A teaching aid in frequent use was the taws, a three-tailed leather strap.

The school quickly acquired a province-wide reputation. One of its outstanding scholars in its early years was Egerton Ryerson who would one day be responsible for education throughout the province. Many of the scholars went on to King's College in York.

Because it was held in rented quarters, the location of the school changed frequently. In the 1840's it was held in a converted stable down a narrow lane off James Street North.

After Mr. Law left to enter the legal profession, a succession of headmasters followed. The most beloved and respected was Dr. John Rae who held this position from the mid-1830's to 1848. He was a graduate in medicine and had a profound interest in science and economics. He introduced and encouraged scientific studies at the district grammar school.

His relationship with his students was rather friendly and casual and on more than one occasion his sense of humour was put to the test by his fun-loving students.

He wore a wig and his students were quick to observe his habit of tilting his chair back and leaning his head against a certain spot on the wall. The spot was coated one day by a daring lad with a thin layer of cobbler's wax. All eyes peered over the tops of the books the next time the headmaster leaned back. The heat of his head softened the wax and, as the students had hoped, when he again sat upright, the wig remained on the wall!

Many sons and grandsons of the local well-to-do acquired a sound education at the Gore District School during the 35 years it operated. But the children of the majority of the citizens even as late as the 1840's still received very little education.

The Common Schools Act of 1816 permitted the erection of a schoolhouse wherever a minimum of 20 pupils could be enrolled. Statistics compiled the following year indicated some 37 common schools in the whole of the District of Gore. Five of these were in Barton. Although their location was not recorded, it is believed that one was on King Street somewhat east of Wellington.

But the number of common schools remained grossly inadequate and only a small percentage of the children attended regularly. The teacher who "boarded round" at the homes of his pupils was often a recent immigrant who only tried his hand at teaching until he could secure a better position.

Dr. Rolph of Ancaster in 1836 found little good to say about the common schools:

It is really melancholy to traverse the Province, and go into many of the common schools; you find a herd of children, instructed by some anti-British adventurer, instilling into the young and tender mind sentiments hostile to the parent state . . . .

(A Brief Account, p. 262)

The 1840's, however, were the era of reform in Upper Canada. Egerton Ryerson became superintendent of education in the province in 1844 and under his leadership over the next three decades, great strides were taken towards free and compulsory education for all.

21

The Old Mill Stream

The subscriber offers for sale his valuable property, well known by the name of the ALBION MILLS . . . with a never failing stream of water running throughout the whole premises.

There are on the premises . . . an extensive Grist Mill, with two pair of stones . . . also a Saw Mill, both of which are in excellent order and in full operation . . . .

Gore Gazette, March 3, 1827

A tedious daily chore for the early settlers was the grinding of corn and wheat into meal and flour. A fortunate few had small milling stones which were turned by hand. Some had to crush the grain with an axe on a flat stone. Others used a hardwood pounder to crush the kernels in the top of a hollowed stump. To make the tiresome job somewhat easier, the pounder was sometimes attached to the end of a branch or sapling which acted as a spring. Some of the bran was removed from the ground grain by putting it through a horse-hair sieve but the bread made from it was coarse and dark. Pioneer housewives longed for the fine stoned flour which only large mills could produce.

A government mill was built in 1783 on 4-Mile Creek near Niagara. By canoe and ox cart and sleigh the settlers made their way to this mill. Some even went on foot carrying a hundred-pound sack of grain on their backs. The trip from the Head of the Lake required at least two days' travel each way.

Privately owned mills soon started to appear beside swiftly flowing streams and waterfalls. Settlements grew around many of these mills. John Green built one at the Forty (Grimsby) in 1789. At one time this mill produced all the flour for the military garrisons of Upper Canada. His brother, Adam, built a crude mill at the foot of the escarpment on Stoney Creek. Another was built in 1791 by Richard Beasley and James Wilson "on a creek that empties into the head of Burlington Bay, near the road leading from said Bay to the Mohawk village." The town of Ancaster gradually grew around this mill and several others were built upstream from it.

Ontario Department of Tourism and Information

(a) INTERIOR, ANCASTER MOUNTAIN MILLS

This view shows the grain being fed into the hopper and then down to the grinding stones which are enclosed in a drum. An uncovered buhr stone appears in the background.

(b) ANCASTER MOUNTAIN MILLS

Erected over a century ago on the site of the first mill at the Head of the Lake, this building houses the last commercially operated mill stones in Canada.

(c) RUINS OF THE DARNLEY GRIST MILL IN CROOKS' HOLLOW

Flour for the British troops in 1813 was ground at this mill on the bank of Spencer Creek.

Lest the settlers be overcharged at these mills, the first parliament of Upper Canada passed an act forbidding millers from taking more than one-twelfth of the settler's grain as a charge for their services. The story is told that one-tenth was the rate being considered but when a miller was asked his opinion, he said that this was not enough. Unfortunately, his ability with numbers did not equal his knowledge of milling. He suggested one-twelfth as a more reasonable amount and this was the figure adopted!

Many millers established a distillery as a profitable sideline. Cheap whiskey was produced from the poorer grades of wheat and from the share the millers gathered as payment.

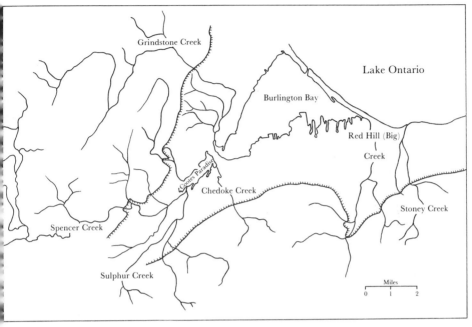

PRINCIPAL WATERSHEDS IN THE HAMILTON AREA
Mills were commonly built on these streams near the edge or base of the escarpment.

There were few streams within Hamilton's present city limits large enough to provide mill sites. An exception was Big Creek where it dropped over the escarpment (Albion Falls). William Davis built a mill there sometime in the 1790's. At a later date when a pit was being quarried for a new waterwheel at the Albion Mills, natural gas was discovered, possibly the first in this part of Ontario. An account of its discovery claimed that two men had been employed to dig the pit into the rock. When one of them stopped to light his pipe, the flame lit the escaping gas. His hair, whiskers and clothing were singed. The two men fled, afraid that they had broken through the earth's crust to the "infernal regions" and that the devil was after them! This gas, despite its unpleasant sulphurous odour, was used to light the mill for many years. Natural gas can still be seen bubbling up through the water in the bed of Red Hill Creek.

Shortly after the turn of the century a skilled millwright by the name of Henry Van Wagner moved to this area from Albany. He settled on the lakeshore on the land that would one day be known as Van Wagner's Beach (now Confederation Park). Many of the mills in Wentworth and adjacent counties were built by him.

In 1832 the assessment lists showed a total of eleven grist mills in those townships which today make up Wentworth County. By then, however, they were outnumbered by thirty-seven saw mills. The demand for sawn lumber had greatly increased as settlers abandoned their log cabins for better homes.

Spencer Creek with its many tributaries rising back in Beverly Swamp was a particularly fine mill stream. Several mills were built near its outlet at the upper end of Cootes Paradise. These mills gave impetus and importance to the community of Dundas. In a three-mile stretch of the creek above Webster's Falls there were once eight damsites which supplied power to several mills. A wide variety of goods in addition to the usual grist and lumber were turned out in the mills along its banks: whiskey, barrels, wool, oatmeal, barley, animal feed, linseed oil, wagon wheels, beer, baskets, axes and cotton. In 1826 the first paper made in this province was produced on the banks of the Spencer in Crooks' Hollow.

Explosions and fires were common occurrences in the early mills which were usually built of wood. These dangers persisted even when they were replaced by towering stone structures, sometimes four and five stories high. The speed of the turning machinery was a constant threat, moreover, to the limbs of the miller and his assistants.

As the forests around the headwaters of the streams were cut down, spring floods became more frequent. Many mills were washed away by cascades of water rushing downstream. In the summer months the flow often dwindled to a mere trickle and the mills sometimes had to close down.

Towards mid-century many owners added steam power to supplement the diminishing supply of water power. But by the end of the century, it had become difficult to compete with the new "manufactories" in the large centres and the mills gradually ceased operation. Little evidence remains today of the scores of mills which once dotted this area.

22

Post Roads and Stage Coaches

Today we leave for Hamilton [from Toronto] papa has hired a sleigh to take us up it was so unpleasant in the stage. We left about ½ past ten & arrived in Hamilton (after a very pleasant drive) at ½ past five.

Sophia MacNab's Diary, March 1, 1846

Several Indian trails traversed these parts before white men settled here. Although the Indians travelled the waterways wherever possible, well-worn paths connected lakes and rivers. Fur traders used these same trails. So did the Loyalist immigrants. An axe was a necessary item of pioneer travel and gradually overhanging branches were removed and the trails were widened.

As early as 1785 a "road" financed by private subscription was blazed from Niagara as far west as Ancaster. But stumps, fallen trees and swamps made such roads virtually impassable for wheeled vehicles. Walking remained the chief means of transportation on land. Most of the produce and supplies were transported in winter when the use of crude sleds pulled by horse, dog or man was possible. From the Indians the settlers learned to use snowshoes.

The parliament of Upper Canada passed legislation in 1793 requiring land owners to open up the road in front of their property. A pathmaster responsible for road construction and maintenance was appointed in each township. Every male was required to work on the roads for a specified number of days each year or make a money payment towards their upkeep. This was known as statute labour.

Governor Simcoe encouraged road building. Several military roads were built under his direction. These also served to open new areas to settlement. The Governor's Road surveyed by Augustus Jones established communication between the lakehead and the Thames River. By 1800 a road was open between Ancaster and Kingston. Early in the new century a road was pushed from the lakehead through Beverly Swamp to Waterloo County for the convenience of the large number of German settlers from Pennsylvania that were flocking there. In the late 1820's the Canada Company opened the Huron Road from Lake Ontario to Lake Huron.

After a route was surveyed, the trees were cut. However, the stumps were usually left in the ground to rot. In swampy sections logs were sometimes laid across the roadbed to make a foundation known as a corduroy road.

In unsettled parts where statute labour was not available, the roads soon fell into a state of disrepair. Underbrush grew up quickly. Mud made travel in the spring months almost impossible. Most travellers continued to use the waterways whenever possible.

By 1827 Ancaster was served by a stage line running from St. Catharines to London. Stage companies at Kingston and York gradually extended their services to this area. In 1833 twice-daily service was inaugurated between Dundas and Hamilton. Five years later regular service to Brantford, Toronto and Niagara was in operation.

The trip to Toronto sometimes took eleven hours! Road conditions made it difficult for the stages to stick to a schedule. The best service was in the winter months when sleighs could be used. In summer months open stages rather than covered coaches were generally used. Numerous accounts were written by early travellers telling of their uncomfortable experiences on these conveyances.

Inns and taverns were as necessary to pioneer travel as service stations, restaurants and motels are today. A few were comfortable establishments, well known for their hospitality and fine food. Too many were notorious for their poor accommodation, their lack of cleanliness and their sickening bill-of-fare. A bribe from the owner of such an establishment, however, often induced a stage driver to stop there. Stage travel was made more hazardous by there being no restrictions against the frequent stops made by some drivers to quench their thirst.

Many well-known inns and taverns existed in Hamilton and the surrounding area. One of the earliest was the King's Head Inn on the lakeshore. Plumer Burley's Hamilton Promenade at the corner of King and James was the place of departure for the local

John Ross Robertson Collection,
Metropolitan Toronto Library Board

Toronto and Early Canadian Picture Collection,
Metropolitan Toronto Library Board

GENERAL STAGE OFFICE, JAMES AND MERRICK, 1855
Carriages such as the one shown here transported passengers to and from the docks at the foot of James Street.

SMITH'S TAVERN, 1850
This tavern dating from before 1800 was on the northwest corner of King and Wellington Streets. Notice the drive shed for horses and carriages.

stages. The Terryberry family operated two inns, one on the Mohawk Road and another on the road to Caledonia. Farmers and wagoners once had their choice of fourteen flourishing hostelries on the road between Hamilton and Caledonia.

The local tavern played an important role in the lives of the early settlers. It was their social centre and meeting place. In more than one community even church services were held there until a more suitable building could be erected. The arrival of a stage at the tavern was an event of considerable excitement. The local inhabitants followed the travellers into the tavern eager to find out what was happening elsewhere. This was often their only source of contact with the rest of the world.

Even the postal service to the pioneer communities of Upper Canada was poor. Before the War of 1812 it was very infrequent and irregular. Weekly service from Montreal to Niagara was introduced after the war. Stages were used to carry the mail whenever possible; couriers on horseback carried it to more remote settlements. In summer months mail was carried on Lake Ontario aboard the steamship *Frontenac*. Hamilton did not get its own post office until 1824.

C. W. Jefferys, Imperial Oil Collection

THE ROYAL MAIL by stagecoach and horses

A letter from England to York took at least two months and sometimes as much as six months. The postal rates were very high. The charge was more than a dollar on a letter to England. Rates were based partially on the number of pages used so most writers wrote very small. After filling the page some even turned it sideways and continued writing across the page. Envelopes were not used; instead, the page was folded and sealed with wax. The postage was usually paid in advance to the postmaster who noted this on the letter. If it was not, it was paid by the receiver. Postage stamps did not come into use in Upper Canada until 1851.

Gradually, as road conditions improved, the mail service got better. A road of four-inch planks laid side by side was built between Hamilton and Caledonia in the early 1840's. It was hailed as a marvel of smoothness—until the winter frosts and spring thaws came! Stone and gravel roadbeds made their appearance. Blacksmith shops became numerous along the roads as horseshoeing became necessary. As roads improved, so did the stages. Covered coaches came into use in the vicinity of the larger towns. By mid-century there were several thousand miles of post roads across the province and a line of mail stages was in daily operation.

23

Canals and Wharves

The subscriber takes this opportunity of informing his friends and the Public in general . . . that he now has four Schooners on Lake Ontario . . . that he has taken every precaution in the selection of sober and industrious men, to be Masters and Crews of said Vessels. . . . The strictest attention will be paid to the delivery of all goods, at any port in Upper Canada on Lake Ontario. . . .

Advertisement by Wm. Chisholm (*Gore Gazette*, July 7, 1827)

The first recorded commercial venture on the shores of Burlington Bay took place in 1669 when La Salle's party exchanged "gifts" with the Indians.

When Mrs. Simcoe and her husband visited this area in 1796 she wrote in her diary that they purchased some fine salmon from Indians fishing in the bay. The Indians gathered at the mouths of the creeks to await the yearly migration of the salmon upstream to spawn. The sand strip was a popular place to camp while they smoked their catch for the months ahead. Any surplus was kept for trade with other tribes.

Commercial activity on the bay shore began in earnest when Richard Beasley established his trading post at Burlington Heights. By 1800 a wharf, one hundred feet long by fifty feet wide, and a sizeable storehouse had been built. There the local Mississauga Indians exchanged furs for the alluring trade goods stocked by Beasley.

Further to the east near the foot of today's Wellington Street, Abel Land built a wharf and carried on a successful shipping business. The chief exports were salt (from Saltfleet Township), potash, whiskey, grain and flour.

In early times the only outlet from the bay to the lake was a shallow natural channel about a quarter mile west of the present canal. Goods were taken across the bay and through the outlet in flat-bottomed bateaux to sailing schooners anchored in the lake.

In 1823 authority was granted for the construction of a canal through the sand strip. While scoffers said that the first storm from the east would fill the channel with sand, workmen, many of them recent immigrants, flocked to the site. Much of the work was done by pick and shovel. Stone to line the canal walls was hauled from the escarpment.

On July 1, 1826, the Burlington Canal was officially opened. The lieutenant-governor and dignitaries of the province passed through in an open boat. They were received at Sherman's wharf by a guard of honour and a military band. An unpublished account of the event, however, stated that the dignity of the occasion was marred by the boat's running aground and the drowning of one of the bandsmen.

After the canal opened there was a hum of activity as wharves and warehouses were built both at the canal and across the bay at the foot of James Street. All was hustle and bustle as a steady stream of ships was loaded and unloaded. Ship building became an important business on the shores of the bay. The hardworking people who made their living on the boats, on the docks and in the shipyards built their homes around the waterfront near the foot of James Street. This was the beginning of the city's colourful "north end," separated in those days from the uptown section by a swamp.

About the time the canal opened, steamships were making their appearance in Upper Canada. In 1829 the *John By*, Hamilton's first steamer, commenced running between Hamilton and Toronto. Under favourable conditions the round trip took only a day! It was little more than a barge equipped with an engine and paddles and drew only two and a half feet of water.

The work of widening, deepening and improving the canal continued over the years as ships became bigger. Tolls were charged for the use of the canal despite protests from merchants and ship owners. People, animals and vehicles were at first ferried across the canal. A swing bridge was in operation a few years later.

A frame lighthouse was erected in 1838 but it was eventually set afire by a spark from a passing steamer. It was replaced in 1859 by

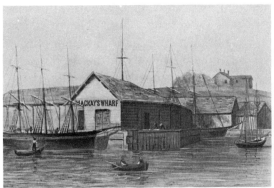 

MacKAY'S WHARF AND WAREHOUSES AT THE FOOT OF JAMES
STREET, 1864

THE BURLINGTON CANAL LIGHTHOUSE
It was built in 1859 to replace an earlier wooden structure which caught on
fire. Although it is still standing (1969), its function has been taken over by
modern navigational equipment.

a stone structure which, although no longer used, still stands
beside the canal.

In the 1840's near where La Salle exchanged gifts with the
Indians, an enterprising man by the name of Alexander Brown
built a large wharf. He secured the contract to supply the wood-
burning steamers of the Ontario Navigation Company with fuel.
Farmers in East Flamborough and neighbouring townships supplemented their incomes by cutting timber and hauling it to
Brown's wharf. The wharf was also the outlet for their excess
produce and the products from Waterdown's mills and quarries.

Meanwhile, Dundas had been struggling to maintain her position as the busiest port at the lakehead. In 1820 a young store
clerk, Peter Desjardins, received government permission to con-
struct a canal from the village through to the marsh in place of
the natural creek outlet then in use. Many years and several government loans were required before the project was finished.
Finally on August 16, 1837, the Desjardins Canal was officially
opened.

For several years it was a busy waterway as a steady flow of produce made its way from the hinterland down the valley to the

Dundas wharves. But the depth of water in the marsh gradually became shallower. The boats kept getting bigger. They could no longer navigate the natural outlet of the marsh into the bay. A channel was cut through Burlington Heights in the 1850's but it did not raise the water level in the marsh, as had been hoped.

From that time forward, Dundas steadily declined in importance as a commercial centre. Hamilton, on the south shore of one of the finest inland harbours in the world, became the chief port and distributing centre for the whole lakehead area.

24

Around Town, 1833

About thirty new buildings of different descriptions are now in progress in this Town, four of which are intended for taverns, and above sixty lots have been sold to be built upon in course of the present and next season, 3 of them for Churches.

Western Mercury, June 7, 1832

After the War of 1812 emigration from the United States into Upper Canada slowed to a trickle but this was offset by an influx of settlers from the British Isles. Many were craftsmen and labourers who were attracted to the communities rather than to the rural areas. Many came here to help with the construction of the Burlington Canal and stayed to work around the waterfront or in the town.

But with the immigrants of 1832 came a scourge. Asiatic cholera swept Europe and Britain that spring. It spread like wildfire in the crowded and unsanitary holds of the immigrant ships. Hundreds were buried at sea. It became commonly known as ship's fever.

When the first shipload of immigrants reached Hamilton that year, citizens of the town were reluctant to let them land for fear that they would spread the disease. George Hamilton, however, persuaded the local residents that it was inhuman to leave the people to die aboard the disease-ridden ships. Crude shelters were built for them on the bay shore. A dilapidated barracks on Burlington Heights, a relic of the War of 1812, became a hospital for the dying. The dead were piled in the nearby military cemetery awaiting burial.

In an effort to ward off the disease, the townspeople cleaned up all refuse from the streets and alleys. Residences and public buildings were scrubbed and disinfected. But the cholera struck. Death usually came to the victim within a day or two of its onset. It claimed one out of every twenty citizens, rich and poor, young and old. Gruesome carts rumbled through the streets, their drivers calling on the inhabitants to bring out their dead. Not until the last ship of the season departed and the cooler weather of autumn arrived did the epidemic wane.

BARTON TOWNSHIP, 1832

Acres of land	
Wild	9394
Arable	6480
Houses	
One story	
square logs	38
framed	114
brick or stone	2
Two story	42
Additional fireplaces	83
Grist mills	1
Saw mills	5
Merchant shops	16
Store houses	6
Horses (three years old and upwards)	314
Oxen (four years old and upwards)	149
Milch cows	547
Young cattle	140
Phaetons	6
Curricles and Gigs	2
Pleasure wagons	23

SOURCE: Page and Smith, *Illustrated Historical Atlas of the County of Wentworth*, p. III.

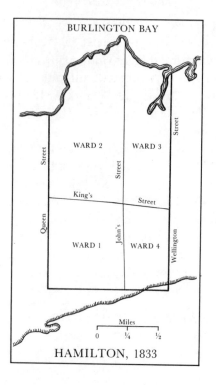

BURLINGTON BAY

WARD 2   WARD 3

King's   Street

WARD 1   WARD 4

Street

Queen

Wellington

Miles

0   ¼   ½

HAMILTON, 1833

But for those not afflicted, life went on in Hamilton. The population had risen to 1400 persons by 1833. A new court house built of stone cut from the escarpment stood across the street from the former log structure. New homes, stores and manufacturing businesses were springing up. Numerous hotels, inns and taverns had been recently erected. Brick buildings were beginning to replace wooden structures. At least three newspapers were published regularly. Stage coach service was available to several centres. The Gore District School continued to attract scholars from across the province. The waterfront was booming. Storekeepers offered for sale a wide choice of quality merchandise, much of it imported.

In the face of such growth, the leaders of the community made application to the provincial assembly for incorporation as a town with authority to administer its own local affairs. Until this time it had been administered as part of the District of Gore. Accordingly, in January, 1833, an act was passed "to define the limits of

ENGINE HOUSE,
KING WILLIAM STREET
The Board of Police which governed the town from 1833 to
1846 met in this building.

John Ross Robertson Collection,
Metropolitan Toronto Library Board

the Town of Hamilton in the District of Gore and to establish a Police and Public Market therein." The boundaries of the town were established as Wellington Street on the east, Queen Street on the west, the bay on the north and the mountain on the south.

A Board of Police was made responsible for the affairs of the town in the same way that the city council is now. The town was divided by "King's" and "John's" Streets into four wards. A representative was elected to the board from each ward. The elected four chose a fifth to serve with them and they then decided among themselves which one would serve as president for that year.

Their duties were numerous. They were responsible for the making of all by-laws affecting the town, the appointment of town officials, the issuing of licenses, fire protection, measures to protect the health and welfare of the citizens, the maintenance of streets and roads, provision of a public market and tax assessment.

Two market sites were available, one on King Street and one on John Street South which George Hamilton was willing to donate. Public opinion favoured the former; the authorities chose the latter. The John Street market served until 1837 by which time a larger market in a more central location was needed. A piece of land west of James and north of York, then an apple orchard, was presented to the town. It still serves as the market place. The John Street market continued in use but only for the sale of such bulky goods as wood and hay.

An examination of a few of the 1833 by-laws in the minute book of the Board of Police shows that some of the problems of that day were not unlike those encountered today. One stated:

. . . every person convicted of having wilfully or negligently suffered his or her hog or hogs, pig or pigs to run at large in the town of Hamilton, shall be liable to a penalty of five shillings for every such hog so suffered to run at large . . . .

Pigs running the streets are no longer a problem but today there are by-laws restricting the running of dogs at large.

Parking and speeding were problems then too. A by-law concerning the obstruction of streets stated:

No Wagon, cart, or carriage of any description, firewood, timber or other incumbrances, shall be allowed to remain in the street for a longer period than twenty-four [hours] . . . .

Another read:

. . . every person who shall ride or drive a horse or horses furiously or immoderately, within the limits of the town of Hamilton, shall be fined, on conviction in a sum not less than two shillings and sixpence nor more than thirty shillings.

Regulations regarding firearms and fireworks are by no means of recent origin for as early as 1833 Hamilton had a by-law prohibiting the firing of "any guns, muskets, or pistols, squibs or fireballs" within the town limits.

Not only did the Board of Police make the laws; they also had to administer them and punish the offenders. But such controls were necessary for by 1834 the population of the growing town had risen to more than 2,000 persons.

25

Sir Allan Napier MacNab

A goodly array of soldiers—say, at least 400 athletic men, with the Honorable Allan MacNab at their head, are now passing our office. . . . Two steamboats are now entering the harbor with Militia from the Gore District.
Toronto Patriot, December 8, 1837

A young man hung out his shingle in 1826 at the northeast corner of King and James Streets to become Hamilton's first resident lawyer. But Allan Napier MacNab was destined for much greater renown on a much wider stage.

He was born in Niagara in 1798, the son of a soldier who had served under Simcoe in the Revolutionary War and who had come to Upper Canada with him as his aide-de-camp. The family soon moved to York where young Allan attended the Home District School.

When the War of 1812 broke out, Allan was only 14 years old. Before it was over, he had served as a militiaman in the defence of York, a sailor on Yeo's flagship and an ensign in the 49th Regiment, thereby earning for himself the name of "Boy Hero" of the war.

While still a teenager, he tried his hand at several occupations including, it is said, those of carpenter and actor. In 1816 he undertook the study of law in the office of the attorney-general. Pursuing his studies intermittently, he was not called to the bar until 1826. During these years he also engaged in several speculative land deals in the York area. This marked the beginning of a lifetime habit of spending money faster than he acquired it. He married but his wife died in 1825.

After her death the young widower moved to Hamilton with his son and infant daughter. His legal business prospered and he was soon able to turn most of the routine work over to his several assistants while he pursued other money-making ventures. He acquired extensive properties in Hamilton and built several houses and stores.

He became a local hero to the people of Hamilton in 1829 when he was jailed for refusing to testify at a parliamentary inquiry into the parading of an effigy of the lieutenant-governor through Hamilton's streets. Shortly thereafter he was elected to the provincial assembly where he represented this area for the next three decades. He became the commander of the local militia. He remarried and became the father of two more daughters, Sophia and Minnie. His purchase of Richard Beasley's property on Burlington Heights allowed him to undertake a long-cherished dream, the building of a home and estate to equal the MacNab ancestral home in Scotland.

All was not good fortune for him, however. His only son was killed in a hunting accident. In 1832 fire broke out in a recently-built tavern owned by him and quickly spread to several other business establishments.

In 1837 occurred the event that brought him prominence throughout the country. MacNab was an avowed Tory, a member of the group that held most of the positions of leadership and responsibility in the province and who were determined that nothing should happen to break up this "Family Compact."

SIR ALLAN NAPIER MacNAB
(From a lithograph of the oil portrait by T. Hamel)

ARRIVAL OF LOYALIST VOLUNTEERS AT PARLIAMENT BUILDINGS, TORONTO, DECEMBER, 1837

The Public Archives of Canada

C. W. Jefferys, Imperial Oil Collection

Opposing them were the Reformers who wanted a greater equality of opportunity in Upper Canada and greater independence from Britain in running its affairs. Some of the more radical Reformers led by William Lyon Mackenzie advocated the use of force to gain their demands as their American brothers had done. Late in 1837 Mackenzie gathered a group of armed followers north of Toronto with the intention of marching on the capital and seizing control of the government.

When news of their activities reached Hamilton, MacNab called out the local militia. Mounted on his favourite horse "Sam Patch" he led the Men of Gore to the waterfront and aboard a Toronto-bound steamship. They joined forces with the regulars and marched north to meet the foe. The rebels were routed in the fiasco which followed.

Mackenzie escaped and made for the border. He reached the Niagara River and established himself on Navy Island. From there he and his supporters hoped to continue the struggle.

Colonel MacNab was put in charge of the troops sent to oust him. They remained at Niagara most of the winter, firing on the island from time to time but they were unable to dislodge Mackenzie. Finally a small force, under orders from MacNab, crossed the river and seized the small steamship Mackenzie used to bring supplies to the island from the United States. Set afire, she plunged over the falls. With her went Mackenzie's ambitions.

Although the destruction of the American-owned ship nearly provoked an international crisis between Britain and America, MacNab was acclaimed a hero and knighted by Queen Victoria.

Sir Allan continued his political career in the assembly. He was twice chosen by his fellow members to be its Speaker. He became the leader of the Tories and served as leader of the opposition throughout much of the 1840's, that era which under moderate Reform leadership brought fundamental changes to the united Canada West (Ontario) and Canada East (Quebec). MacNab played his part in ensuring that reforms were not carried so far that the ties with Britain were threatened.

In 1854 MacNab's party returned to power. MacNab thus became the prime minister. Several measures of economic advantage to the country were introduced under him. After just two years in office, ill health forced him to relinquish the post to the youthful John A. Macdonald.

Throughout his years in government he still continued to be a dominant personality on the local scene. He at some time served as president or director of nearly every important company and institution in Hamilton. He was an active member of many local organizations.

Railways were his greatest interest. Long before most others, he realized their importance to the commercial and industrial growth of our city. It was he who laid the industrial foundations of our city when he had the Great Western Railway routed along the Hamilton waterfront rather than through Dundas.

A man of firm convictions, he had his critics and enemies. But to his friends and supporters he was a genial and fun-loving companion, a charming and gracious host, a kind and loving father, a benevolent and public-spirited Hamiltonian, a witty and persuasive speaker and a shrewd politician. No other Upper Canadian was more actively involved in so many of the major military, political, economic and social events of that era.

26

Dundurn

And Papa not wishing to be out done immediately got the steps and got up into the tree, he through us down lots of Cherries and also met with a great many adventures, he stained his shirt sleeve with Cherries, he tore his coat sleeve nearly half out and got some Cherries juice on his coat, and as a finale he sat down on a lot of Cherries—

Sophia MacNab's Diary, July 6, 1846

Richard Beasley made many improvements to his property on Burlington Heights over the years he resided there. A brick cottage, said to be the first such building at the lakehead, replaced his earlier, more humble dwelling. But he continued to be pressed for money and was finally forced to sell the property.

Allan MacNab, the rising young lawyer and politician, purchased it in 1832. Shortly thereafter he commenced construction of Dundurn. The light-coloured stucco mansion was built around Beasley's cottage. It was built in the Regency style, a style of architecture new to North America. Battlements and two Italianate turrets adorned the roof. Its floor-length French windows permitted easy access to terraces and gardens. MacNab set out to own the finest home west of Montreal; in this he succeeded. The mansion was ready for occupancy about 1835 but work on it continued throughout MacNab's lifetime.

Dundurn contained about fifty rooms. The main ones on the ground floor were the entrance hall with its carved walnut hanging staircase, the elegant drawing room where dances were often held, the grand and formal dining room overlooking the gardens and Burlington Bay, a library, a smoking room, sitting rooms and serving rooms. Built into the wall of the dining room was the triple-doored vault where family valuables were kept. On the floor above were the bedrooms and sitting rooms for the family and guests. One room was set aside as a school room for MacNab's daughters who were tutored at home.

107

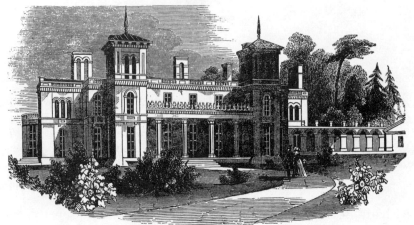

DUNDURN, 1849 (north side) *Illustrated London News* (April 28, 1849)

But much of the everyday life at Dundurn was in the basement where the servants' quarters were. A staff of ten or more was responsible for the upkeep of the home. They worked sixteen hours a day and received little remuneration except room and board. They were permitted a half day off a month. Also in the basement were the spacious kitchen, wash house, well room, scullery, dairy, ice house, brewery, wine cellar and storage rooms.

Formal gardens, imposing gates, a family burial plot, stables and a picturesque dovecote were added to the grounds. The original purpose of a small octagonal building to the east of the castle was for years a mystery. It has since been identified as a cockpit. Cockfighting was very popular in MacNab's day. The men gathered after dinner and sat on the benches around the inside of the building while the cocks battled in the shallow pit in the centre of the floor. Around the edge of the property were Castle Dean where the supervisor of the estate lived, Battery Lodge, which served as the gatekeeper's house, and the gardener's residence.

Ever the gracious host, MacNab loved to entertain. Visitors to Dundurn were numerous. After the death of his second wife, his sister-in-law, Sophia, took over the running of the household. Great festivities attended the weddings of his daughters. In 1860

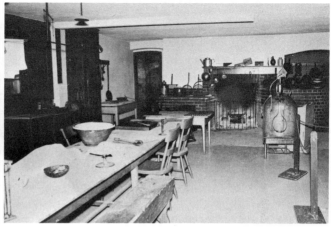

THE LIBRARY
AT DUNDURN

DUNDURN'S KITCHEN
Here in the basement, the food for the castle's occupants
and visitors was prepared.

he entertained the Prince of Wales at luncheon. But so lavish a
way of life was expensive. Dundurn was heavily mortgaged and
local shopkeepers and tradesmen often had to wait many months
for payment of Dundurn accounts.

After MacNab's death, the furnishings of Dundurn were sold
by auction and the house stood vacant for a couple of years. It
then served for a time as the provincial school for the deaf. In
the 1870's it was purchased by Donald McInnes, a local senator,
who used it as a residence. Some changes and renovations were
made. But he also found Dundurn expensive to maintain. The
public were permitted to use the grounds for recreational and
sporting activities to help pay for its upkeep.

About the turn of the century Dundurn was purchased by the
city of Hamilton. The mansion became a museum. Over the years
it became the storehouse and display case for a vast collection of
miscellanea donated by local citizens. The beauty of the castle
lay hidden behind the clutter of these exhibits.

But in the mid-1960's Dundurn again took on its former splen-
dour. Its restoration became the official centennial project of the
city of Hamilton. Under expert guidance every effort was made
to restore the castle to its grandeur of the 1850's when MacNab
was prime minister.

Layers of paint were removed to find traces of the original paint and wallpaper. In the process, fireplaces, windows and even rooms which had been covered over were discovered. Extensive work was necessary in the basement. For over a hundred years many Hamiltonians had believed that tunnels radiated from the basement to various parts of the grounds but not a trace of evidence was found to substantiate this myth. However, a wall of Beasley's brick cottage was found.

The committee responsible for the furnishings spent months searching through attics and antique shops for suitable pieces. The search even extended to Britain where MacNab may have bought some of the original furniture. Individuals and organizations donated money towards the purchase of needed articles. At last after three years of intensive research and labour, MacNab's beloved Dundurn was again ready to receive visitors.

DUNDURN, 1969 (south side)

27

When the Fire Bell Rang

. . . each and every tenant or occupant of a dwelling house in the town of Hamilton shall provide one or more good and suitable leathern buckets, holding not less than three gallons each, with the owner's name marked thereon, which shall be kept in readiness to assist in extinguishing fires, under a penalty of not less than five nor more than thirty shillings.

By-Law 5, Town of Hamilton
March 18, 1833

Citizens of the infant settlement at the Head of the Lake lived in constant fear of fire. Wooden houses heated by wood-burning fireplaces and stoves presented a serious fire hazard. Upon hearing the dreaded cry "Fire!" or upon seeing flames shooting from a neighbour's dwelling, everyone grabbed a bucket and rushed to the scene. Often, however, there was not a sufficient supply of water at hand and their efforts to save the building were usually futile.

On a blustery autumn day in 1832, fire broke out in a tavern in the heart of the town. The flames, fanned by the wind, quickly spread to five other business establishments, including the post office and the offices of the Desjardins Canal Company and the *Western Mercury*. Within three hours the buildings were completely destroyed.

It is therefore understandable why fire protection was a matter of great concern to the Board of Police which governed the town from 1833 to 1846. Three by-laws concerning fire protection were passed at one of their earliest meetings in 1833.

In addition to being required to have a "leathern bucket" always at hand, each householder was required to have a permanently fixed ladder to the roof and another to each chimney that rose more than four feet above the roof. Since many fires resulted from the accumulation of soot in a chimney becoming ignited, chimneys were inspected regularly.

111

A town chimney sweep was later employed. Chimneys and stoves in regular use had to be cleaned monthly. The charge was 7½ pence for sweeping a chimney and one shilling for cleaning stove pipes. As a further precaution against fires, citizens were not allowed to carry burning coals from one house to another except in a covered container. Fines were levied against persons who failed to comply with these regulations. The Board of Police also authorized the digging of five wells, each containing five feet of water, at convenient locations about the town.

In 1834 the purchase of a fire "engine" and a place where it could be kept were considered. This piece of apparatus which was essentially just a hand pump on wheels arrived the next year. The cost, including several feet of hose and freight charges, was less than $800. The manufacturer guaranteed its performance for two years, if given proper care.

A piece of land on the north side of King William Street between John and Hughson was donated by a prominent citizen on condition that it always be used for an engine house or some other related purpose. Offices of the fire department still occupy the site.

The first volunteer engine company was formed early in 1836. When a fire broke out, the town fire bell was rung. The members of the engine company left their work and ran to the engine house. The engine was dragged to the fire. While four men manned the long handles of the pump, the others directed the stream of water from the leather hoses onto the flames. These volunteers received no pay. Their uniform at first consisted only of a cap and belt supplied at public expense.

Citizens were also required to give their assistance at fires if demanded. The tank on the engine had to be kept filled with water. A money reward was given to the first citizen to arrive at the fire with a barrel of water. At night young lads bearing torches led the fire company to the fire and furnished light at the scene.

As more engines were purchased and more companies formed, the first company to arrive at a blaze was given a cash award. Later, each company also received a fixed amount for each fire it attended. But engines and equipment were costly and these were

Ontario Archives

EARLY HAMILTON FIRE "ENGINE"
The long handles were used to pump water
from the tank through the hose.

EARLY FIREFIGHTING
EQUIPMENT
(Westfield Pioneer Village)

often purchased from funds which the men of the company donated or raised themselves.

Prominent businessmen also sometimes donated engines and equipment. In 1843 John Fisher, the owner of a foundry on James Street North, built and donated a fire engine for public use. It was housed at his foundry just across the street from the Gore District Grammar School. It must have been very difficult for the boys to concentrate on their studies when they heard the clang of the fire bell and the thud of running feet.

Mr. Fisher's engine which was capable of pumping 60 gallons of water a minute has been carefully preserved. It still makes occasional public appearances, usually in parades along with a modern pumper capable of delivering hundreds of gallons per minute.

By 1854 the fire brigade consisted of one hook-and-ladder company, one hose company and four engine companies. At the time of Confederation there was an engine house in every ward of the city. The volunteer brigade served the community until 1879.

Bibliography

Part V (1815-1846)

Bailey, T. Melville, *The History of Dundurn Castle and Sir Allan MacNab,* Hamilton, 1943.

Bailey, T. Melville, *The Laird of Dundurn,* Hamilton, 1968.

Carter, Charles and Bailey, T. Melville (ed.), *The Diary of Sophia MacNab,* Hamilton, Griffin, 1968.

Charlton, R. S., "Administrative Beginnings in the Town of Hamilton," *Wentworth Bygones,* II, (1960), pp. 2-15.

Durand, Charles, *Reminiscences of Charles Durand of Toronto, Barrister,* Toronto, Hunter, Rose, 1897.

Edwards, Nina L., "The Establishment of Papermaking in Upper Canada," *Ontario History,* XXXIX, (1947), pp. 63-74.

Gore Gazette, March 3, 1827-June 8, 1829, on microfilm, Hamilton Public Library.

Gourlay, Robert, *Statistical Account of Upper Canada,* Vol. I, London, Simpkin & Marshall, 1822.

Guillet, Edwin, *Pioneer Inns and Taverns,* 5 vol., Toronto, 1954-1962.

Guillet, Edwin, *Pioneer Days in Upper Canada,* Toronto, University of Toronto Press, 1963.

Guillet, Edwin, *Pioneer Travel in Upper Canada,* Toronto, University of Toronto Press, 1963.

Guillet, Edwin, *The Story of Canadian Roads,* Toronto, University of Toronto Press, 1966.

Howison, John, *Sketches of Upper Canada,* Edinburgh, Oliver & Boyd, 1821.

James, R. Warren, *John Rae, Political Economist, Vol. I. Life and Miscellaneous Writings,* Toronto, University of Toronto Press, 1965, pp. 43-63.

Jehan, D. A., *A Century of Service, Hamilton Fire Department, 1867-1967,* Hamilton, 1967.

Lemon, Agnes H., "Biographical Sketch of a Noted Pioneer," *Wentworth Historical Society Papers and Records,* II, (1899), pp. 136-139.

McKenzie, Thos. H., "Topographical Sketch of Hamilton as it was in 1830 and 1881," *Wentworth Historical Society Papers and Records,* I, (1892), pp. 178-181.

Provincial Statutes of Upper Canada, Revised, Collected and Republished by Authority, York, R. C. Horne, 1818.

Rolph, Dr. Thomas, *A Brief Account, Together with Observations, Made during a Visit in the West Indies, and a Tour through the United States of America, in parts of the years 1832-3; Together with a Statistical Account of Upper Canada,* Dundas, Hackstaff, 1836.

Thomson, Thomas M., *The Spencer Story,* Hamilton, Spencer Creek Conservation Authority, 1965, pp. 13-22.

Turner, J. E., "Albion Mills," *Wentworth Bygones,* III, (1962), pp. 10-16.

Wentworth Historical Society, "Report of the Burlington Bay Canal Commissioners for 1835," *Papers and Records,* II, (1899), pp. 168-170.

Woodhouse, T. Roy, "The Beginnings of the History of Hamilton," *Wentworth Bygones,* V, (1964), pp. 23-27.

Part VI

. . . the ambitious and
stirring little city

1845	Board of Trade formed
1846	*population 6,832*
	Hamilton Spectator begins publication
1847	Hamilton becomes a city; Colin Ferrie first mayor
	council meetings in James Street market house
	Canada Life Asssurance Company
1848	free vaccination of children against smallpox
	orphanage established by Ladies' Benevolent Society
1849	public cemetery on Burlington Heights
1852	Sisters of St. Joseph establish convent here
1853	Central School opened
1854	Great Western Railway
	cholera epidemic
1856	*population 21,855*
1857	Desjardins Canal disaster
1859	first elected mayor
	G.W.R. shops located here
	last public hanging
1860	Prince of Wales visits city
	Provincial Agricultural Exhibition at Crystal Palace
1862	depression; city bankrupt
	death of MacNab
	formation of 13th Battalion, Volunteer Militia
1866	*population 21,485*
1867	Confederation; Hamilton's Samuel Mills appointed to Senate

28

Hamilton Becomes a City

Excellent freestone and limestone are procured from the mountain, which are of great advantage to the town, as the merchants are beginning to build almost exclusively of stone; and the town promises in a few years to become one of the handsomest on the continent of America.

Smith's Canadian Gazeteer, 1846, (p. 75)

The prospect of becoming the business capital for the western part of the province came to Hamilton with the opening of the Burlington Canal in 1826 and the Welland Canal a few years later.

As ships of the day became larger, they were no longer able to navigate "Desjardin's Ditch" to Dundas and docked instead at Hamilton. Exports from Hamilton mounted steadily. Wharf and warehouse facilities underwent continuous expansion.

There developed in Hamilton and the surrounding area a growing market for those goods not produced locally. Wholesalers, realizing the importance of Hamilton's location, set up flourishing businesses here. Prominent among them were Colin Ferrie and Isaac Buchanan, two men who were to contribute much, both economically and politically, to the city's development.

The completion of the plank road through Caledonia to Port Dover opened up communication between Hamilton and the settlements on the lower Grand River and Lake Erie. Plans were under consideration for a railway southward to Lake Erie and another westward to London.

James Street was opened to the top of the mountain. Farmers were able to bring their produce from the hinterland down James Street to the docks. When the steeper access road at John Street was abandoned, James Street replaced John Street as the commercial centre of the city.

Banking facilities were needed in the flourishing business community. With MacNab's assistance and influence, the Gore Bank was established here. Although the subject of much criticism in its early years, as time passed and many rival banks failed, it acquired a very reliable reputation. Many local enterprises, both private and public, were financed with loans from its coffers.

The young manager of another local bank became interested in the recently established practice of insuring one's life but found upon investigation that he would have to travel to New York to do so. So Hugh Cossart Baker decided to start a Canadian insurance company and thus it was in Hamilton that the Canada Life Assurance Company was formed.

In 1845 several prominent businessmen met at a local hotel and formed a board of trade, similar to today's Chamber of Commerce, for the purpose of promoting and encouraging local business development.

As James Street became the business centre of the city, nearby York Street became the home of many of the city's prominent

HAMILTON, 1846

PROFESSIONS AND TRADES

9	physicians and surgeons	3	watchmakers
16	lawyers	6	bakers
3	breweries	10	shoemakers
10	wholesale importers	3	gunsmiths
	(dry goods and groceries)	3	confectioners
5	importers (hardware)	14	groceries
49	stores	11	beer shops
2	foundries	6	builders
4	printing offices	5	stone masons
3	booksellers	5	tinsmiths
3	chemists	4	hatters
65	taverns	14	tailors
2	tanneries	8	painters
3	coachmakers	1	marble and stone works
2	soap and candle factories	13	blacksmiths
4	auctioneers	3	ladies' seminaries
5	saddlers	2	schools for boys
11	cabinet makers	4	banks

SOURCE: *Smith's Canadian Gazeteer*, p. 76.

and well-to-do businessmen. Fine residences, many of them built of stone, bordered the street. Dominating all of them at the end of the street, was MacNab's Dundurn.

The business boom that had come to Hamilton was reflected in the population growth. From less than 3,000 a decade earlier, the population had increased to nearly 7,000 in 1846. Neighbouring communities quipped that in order to reach that figure the town officials must have included the residents of the local cemeteries or taken the count on a day when the town was crowded with visitors.

But the town fathers thought the time had come to press for city status. The necessary legislation was completed and on January 1, 1847, Hamilton officially became a city. The boundaries were extended to Emerald Street on the east and Paradise Road on the west.

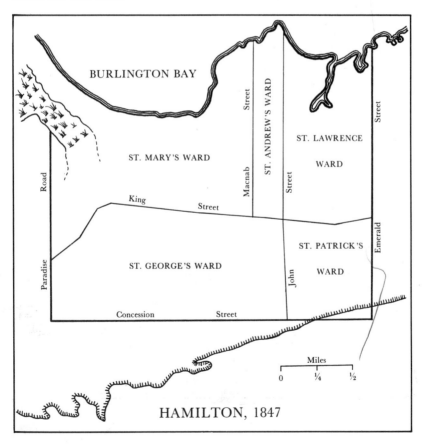

The Board of Police which had administered the town since its incorporation was replaced by a mayor and council. A fifth ward was created and the wards were named after patron saints instead of merely being numbered. Each ward elected two councillors. These ten chose an eleventh councillor and then the eleven chose one from amongst themselves to serve as mayor. Colin Ferrie who had served on the first Board of Police in 1833 became Hamilton's first mayor.

Meetings of the council were held in the market hall on James Street, henceforth to be known as the city hall. On the upper floor there was an open hall with a stage at one end. It had been used for meetings and diverse entertainments including plays, dances, debates and boxing matches. Even dancing bears had performed there. The hall was converted to a council chamber with furnishings removed from the engine house on King William Street. Meat, eggs, butter and other produce continued to be sold on the ground floor and in the basement.

Changes in the administration of the Gore District were also

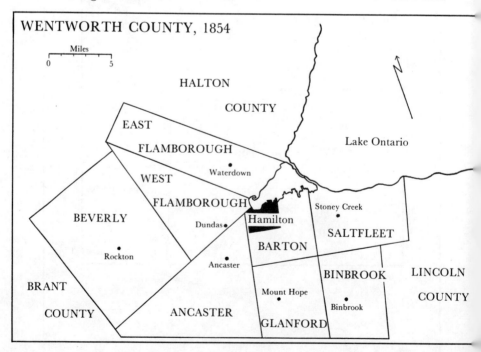

WENTWORTH COUNTY, 1854

occurring. District councils were established in 1841 to replace the obsolete quarter session courts which had administered the districts up to that time. Councillors were elected by the rate-payers of each township but the warden and treasurer were appointed by the governor.

However, the Gore District proved to be much too large for effective administration. In 1851 the townships in the southwest part of the district were combined to form the separate county of Brant. Wentworth and Halton separated in 1854. The townships of Ancaster, Barton, Beverly, Binbrook, Glanford, Saltfleet, East Flamborough and West Flamborough became the constituent parts of Wentworth County.

29

The Power of the Press

Wood, Butter, and Hams, will be taken in payment for Subscription to the Gore Gazette, if soon delivered at this office.

Gore Gazette, September 1, 1827

Feathers, of a Good Quality, will be received for subscription to the Gore Gazette—if soon delivered at this office.

Gore Gazette, October 6, 1827

Newspapers likely became common at the Head of the Lake about 1800 when Richard Beasley became the local agent for the *Canadian Constellation* published at Niagara. Charles Durand claimed that his father was the owner of a paper in 1812 in which General Brock inserted his proclamation of the war. Durand was still living at the Head of the Lake then but no proof of the paper's local existence has been found. Publication of a Dundas newspaper is said to have commenced in 1818.

CITY HALL, JAMES STREET   Head-of-the-Lake Historical Society
Built originally as a market house, this building served as the city hall from
1847 to 1889.

A newspaper with the somewhat lengthy name, the *Gore Gazette and Ancaster, Hamilton, Dundas and Flamborough Advertiser,* was started in Ancaster in 1827. Although it was published for only two years, copies of this paper which have been preserved on microfilm are an invaluable source of information about early times in this area. Its first issue ran an advertisement for stone cutters and stone masons for the new court house.

The honour of being Hamilton's first newspaper is given to the *Gore Balance* (1829-1830). By 1833 Hamilton had three weekly newspapers, the *Hamilton Free Press,* the *Western Mercury* and the *Canadian Wesleyan,* as well as several twice-monthly literary journals. In the late 1830's and 1840's a number of other newspapers appeared in Hamilton. Most of these early newspapers appeared weekly. They usually consisted of a single sheet, folded in half to make four pages. The majority of them were short-lived, some only lasting a few weeks.

The printing of a newspaper required the selection of the needed letters from trays of type. The letters were placed in holders to produce lines of type. The flatbed presses were hand-operated. Considerable strength was required and the muscles of the pressman's right shoulder usually became much developed. His right foot, braced on the frame of the press, also became enlarged. As a result, many printers acquired a manner of walking that was a mark of their trade.

An apprentice was usually given the messy job of applying ink to the type, a job which had to be done for every copy. The printing ink was made from lampblack and varnish. The paper that was fed through the presses was made from rags. At first it had to be imported from England or the United States. It became available locally after James Crooks started to manufacture paper in 1826 at his mill on Spencer Creek in West Flamborough.

Many of the early newspapers were produced by only one man who had to be his own reporter, editor, typesetter, pressman, salesman and business manager. A considerable amount of money was needed to acquire a shop and the necessary equipment. Competition was keen with so many papers in existence. Circulation was usually only a few hundred copies of each issue. The average cost of a year's subscription was 20 shillings, payable in cash or produce. Publishers often had difficulty collecting payment. Postage rates were high if the paper had to be mailed to the subscriber. It is little wonder that so many papers ceased publication after a very short existence. To supplement their meagre incomes, most publishers also did job printing of posters, notices, handbills, pamphlets and even books.

Because they only appeared weekly, the early newspapers did not contain a great deal of local news. That circulated faster by word of mouth. But news from Britain and other countries was avidly read, even though it was several weeks old. Advertisements filled a considerable amount of space. Poems, often written by local subscribers, were also numerous.

The most popular feature, however, was the editorial which was usually written by the owner of the newspaper. In it he gave free expression to his own opinion. Most of the time it was about

PRINTING PRESS,
WESTFIELD
PIONEER VILLAGE
It was on a press
similar to this that the
Hamilton Spectator
was first printed.

the affairs of government. Some editors were strong in their support of those in power, perhaps in the hope that it might bring them some government printing jobs. Others attacked the province's leaders in a manner which today would involve them in endless lawsuits for libel.

The subscribers were eager to read what their favourite editor had to say. For those who could not read, there was always someone in the local tavern who was only too happy to relay the contents for that week, or his own version of it. Since the same subject might be differently described by rival editors, arguments and even brawls were numerous on the days the papers were published. Politics was indeed a popular sport of the day.

It was from this love of politics that the *Hamilton Spectator* was born. A group of local men wanted a newspaper more moderate in outlook than the very conservative *Hamilton Gazette*. A young master printer by the name of Robert Reid Smiley was enticed to come to Hamilton. Above a drug store on James Street North, he published the first edition of the *Spectator and Journal of Commerce* on July 15, 1846, on a secondhand press capable of turning out 200 copies an hour.

Its subscribers gradually grew in number from hundreds to thousands and it became a daily. By 1856 its publishers claimed it to have the largest circulation of any Canadian newspaper west of Toronto.

Over the years it had stiff competition from many papers, notably from the *Times* and *Herald*. All of these eventually bowed out leaving the *Spectator* the sole survivor on the local scene.

30

The Central School

Let us go into the library. Do you remember how the shivers used to go up and down your back when you saw the skeleton?

Miss A. M. Hamilton, 1927 Central Reunion
(*Hamilton Spectator,* June 30, 1927)

A new era in education in Canada West dawned with the appointment of Egerton Ryerson as its chief superintendent in 1844. Under his leadership measures were introduced over the next three decades which gave this province wide acclaim for its fine educational system.

Education was made compulsory. Financial support for schools came increasingly from grants and property taxes instead of from fees. Teacher training was introduced. Courses of study were standardized. Textbooks written by Canadians were provided. Sturdy schools of brick or stone replaced the log and frame structures of an earlier era. Hamilton gave support to, and leadership in, many of these developments.

The Board of Police had been responsible for education when Hamilton was a town. The town was divided into five common school districts. Classes were held in rented quarters and their location changed frequently, sometimes several times even in the course of a year.

After Hamilton became a city, an appointed Board of Trustees was made responsible for education in the city. The trustees requested a report from the district superintendent of schools to assist them in their planning. It revealed that there were over two thousand children of school age in Hamilton but there were only six common schools with accommodation for some 350 pupils. Average daily attendance was considerably less. Some children attended the Gore District Grammar School and private schools in the city but it was obvious to the trustees that a vast number of children in the city were not attending school at all.

Controversy raged as to how to provide the best education for the greatest number of children. Some wanted a common school in each ward. Others wanted one multi-roomed school in the central part of the city. Finally after much debate and study, the latter scheme was adopted.

A site was chosen. For an outlay of £1000 the Board of Education of Hamilton acquired its first property, a two-acre plot on a rise on the south side of Hunter Street between Park and Bay Streets. An attractive two-storied, twelve-roomed stone structure capable of accommodating a thousand scholars was erected.

The spacious building had good heating and ventilating systems. The well-lit classrooms were equipped with proper furniture, blackboards, maps, globes and textbooks. There was a large assembly room on the second floor and separate playgrounds for boys and girls.

It was officially opened on May 2, 1853, with appropriate ceremonies. However, the special guests, Rev. Dr. Ryerson and the headmaster of the normal school in Toronto, did not arrive in time for the event and the *Spectator* of the following day reported, "The proceedings at the opening were rather flat on the whole."

Nevertheless the Central School was an important landmark in the educational history of this province:

Ontario Archives

CENTRAL SCHOOL, BUILT 1853
(From *Canadian Illustrated News,* May 16, 1863) The clock tower which now adorns the building was added at a later date.

This is the first representative institution in the Province of a properly graded common school, in which were separate rooms, separate teachers and separate classes, presided over by a competent principal, who directed the energies of pupils and teachers along well defined lines.
(Smith, *The Central School,* p. 7)

Educators and men of influence throughout the province watched with keen interest. Visitors came from distant places to see it.

It also had its critics. More than one person predicted its failure. One group, certain that it would soon close its doors, began negotiations to purchase the building and site.

But under the supervision of J. H. Sangster, its twenty-two-year-old principal, and a very capable staff, the school was a success from the beginning. Some 600 boys and girls initially enrolled and the number steadily grew. The well-to-do were at first reluctant to send their children to it because they did not want them mixing with the "riffraff" of the city. This reluctance disappeared when the excellence of its instruction became known.

The Central School was originally an elementary school. In 1854 a classical department was added and two years later the Gore District Grammar School amalgamated with it. Children from outside the city were admitted upon payment of fees. By 1858 the school was overcrowded. The practice of having primary schools in each ward serving as feeders to the Central School was introduced. These primary or ward schools were under the charge and direction of the principal of the Central School. Over-crowding continued at Central and a separate senior grammar school was erected in 1866 at the corner of Main and Caroline.

Ontario Archives

PUPILS OF THE CENTRAL SCHOOL AT MILITARY DRILL
(From *Canadian Illustrated News,* February 14, 1863)

In 1867 the comprehensive course of instruction at the Central School included reading, writing, arithmetic, geography, grammar, history (Canadian, English and general), linear drawing, book-keeping, human philosophy, astronomy, elements of natural philosophy and chemistry, algebra, Euclid, mensuration, trigonometry, natural history, botany and geology. A charge of twenty-five cents a month was made to cover the costs of books and stationery. Its library to which the pupils had free access contained 1400 volumes.

Most of the pupils worked hard to earn the special certificate for "diligence and good conduct" presented upon leaving the school. Central's "old boys and old girls" went on to all walks of life carrying with them fond memories of their school days there.

31

The Coming of the Iron Horse

Railways are my politics.

Sir Allan MacNab, 1853

January 19, 1854, was a public holiday in Hamilton. Flags and streamers decorated the streets and buildings. A tumultuous parade passed under a triumphal arch at King and James. The mayor of Hamilton gamboled up the centre of the street arm in arm with the mayor of Rochester. The fair maidens of the city waved and fluttered their handkerchiefs from windows and balconies above. The Great Western Railway from Niagara Falls to Windsor was finished! The railway era had come to Hamilton.

As early as 1834 a charter had been granted for the construction of a railway from Burlington Bay to London. As no work had been undertaken ten years later, the charter was amended. The line was to run from Niagara to Windsor. The name was changed to the Great Western Railway. Original plans had the line skirting Hamilton on top of the escarpment but through the influence of MacNab, it was brought along the south shore of the bay.

Construction began in 1851. Rails and equipment had to be brought from Britain. The work was done by pick, shovel and wheelbarrow. Parts of the line were opened to traffic late in 1853.

At 2 A.M. on January 17, 1854, the first through train stopped in Hamilton on its way from Niagara Falls to Windsor. Although official celebrations were scheduled for two days later, hundreds of Hamiltonians were on hand to cheer its arrival at the station. So many local citizens wanted to climb aboard for the historic trip that a second train of twelve coaches was hurriedly pressed into service.

Following ceremonies at Windsor and Detroit, it was Hamilton's turn when the trains made their return trip on January 19. The climax of the local celebration was a gala ball sponsored by the railway company. Some 1500 ladies and gentlemen from all parts of the province and the United States danced from nine o'clock to dawn.

Absent from these festive activities, however, was the president of the Great Western. Sir Allan MacNab was confined to bed at Dundurn with a cold. A delegation marched to Dundurn where the artillery fired a twenty-one-gun salute in his honour. In following years he had the satisfaction of being able to stand on his balcony and watch the trains sweeping around the curve of the bay shore into the city.

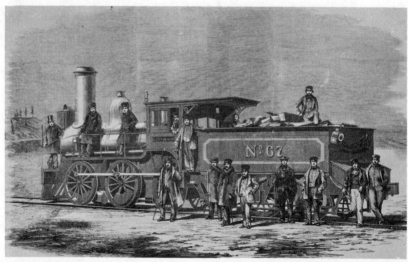

EARLY LOCOMOTIVE   *Illustrated London News* (September 1, 1860)
This engine was built in Hamilton for the Great Western Railway.

DESJARDINS CANAL DISASTER, 1857

The first locomotives were imported from England and United States. Like ships, each bore its own distinctive name. Some of the early freight engines from England had such descriptive names as *Rhinoceros, Hippopotamus* and *Elephant.* The Daniel C. Gunn engine shop on Wellington Street North produced the first Canadian-built locomotives in 1856.

The early engines with their tall smoke stacks burned wood. Frequent stops at the huge piles along the track were necessary. Many area farmers added to their incomes by cutting fuel for the railway. Coal came into use in the 1860's but it was disliked by many engineers who prided themselves on the cleanliness and shine of their engines. It was also said that pieces of wood were handier than hunks of coal to throw at cows that strayed onto the track.

Construction of a line from Hamilton to Toronto was completed in 1855. The daily express made the trip with a stop at Oakville in just one hour and twenty-eight minutes!

Three years after its joyous opening, the Great Western suffered a dreadful disaster which had a grave effect on Hamilton. On March 12, 1857, the late afternoon passenger train from Toronto crashed through the swing bridge over the Desjardins

Canal on Burlington Heights. The next issue of the *Spectator* reported:

... the engine, tender, baggage car and two first-class passenger cars broke through the severed frame work, and leaped, headlong, into the yawning abyss below. The engine and tender crashed at once through the ice. The baggage car, striking the corner of the tender in the act of falling, was thrown to one side and fell some ten yards from the engine. The first passenger car rushed after, and, turning as it descended, fell on its roof, breaking partly through the ice, and being crushed to atoms, while the last car fell endways on the ice, and, strange to say, remained in that position.

Of the hundred or so passengers, fifty-nine persons lost their lives. Several prominent Hamiltonians were among them. Only four persons in the first car survived.

People flocked to the scene. The rescuers toiled through the night and into the next day. March 16 was proclaimed a day of mourning and prayer. All businesses were closed. Services were held in churches throughout the city which was draped in black. Church bells tolled for hours as the long funeral processions made their way to the cemetery only a short distance from where the disaster occurred.

A careful investigation was made. The engine was raised from the canal. A broken axle which threw the engine from the rails was found to have caused the tragedy. The bridge was not strong enough to withstand the impact of the derailed engine.

GREAT WESTERN RAILWAY SHOPS
(From *Canadian Illustrated News,* February 14, 1863)

By 1860 the Great Western had, in addition to the main line running from the Niagara River to the Detroit River, several branch lines in the southwestern part of the province. Stage coaches provided local service from the numerous stops along the routes.

In Toronto connections could be made with the Grand Trunk for rail transportation to Montreal and the Atlantic coast. Rail service was also available via Windsor and the Michigan Central to Chicago. One could travel from Hamilton to New York City by way of Niagara Falls and the New York Central. Hamilton was indeed at the hub of a vast railway network. Wholesaling establishments in Hamilton flourished as imported goods were sent on the railway from Hamilton into the heartland of southwestern Ontario. It in turn sent its produce to Hamilton for forwarding to distant markets.

In 1859 the Great Western set up shops in Hamilton for the building and repairing of locomotives. Four years later a rolling mill was put into operation to reroll the English rails which easily broke in the harsh Canadian winters.

The Great Western is credited with the construction of the world's first sleeping car. The plan was developed by Samuel Sharp, the master-mechanic of the railway. It had a double row of berths, three tiers high, running through the centre of the car. George Pullman, the American inventor whose name has become synonymous with railway sleeping cars, is said to have been influenced by Sharp's design.

Ontario Archives

The Great Western Railway was a very important factor in Hamilton's growth as a manufacturing city. Immigrants who helped with its construction swelled the city's population. The locomotive shops and rolling mill provided employment for hundreds of local residents. With all of southwestern Ontario as a potential market, other manufacturing establishments blossomed and grew in Hamilton.

32

Immigrants and Epidemics

Those with families should especially take care that their children have been vaccinated before leaving home, as the small pox has been known to have been taken on board a ship and produced great ravages among the crew.

Dr. Thomas Rolph, 1836
(*A Brief Account*, p. 118)

Immigrants continued to flock to Canada West from Great Britain throughout the middle decades of the nineteenth century.

Some were retired soldiers who had served in Canada with the British army. Their meagre pension could be made to go further here than in Britain. Others were soldiers who had served in the campaigns against Napoleon in Europe and were unable to find employment upon their return to Britain.

Many immigrants were skilled hand craftsmen who had been put out of work by the rise of factories in the industrial revolution that was sweeping England. From Scotland came thousands who had been evicted from their little crofts by landowners eager to turn Scotland into a huge sheep pasturage to feed the looms in English factories. Most numerous of all were the Irish immigrants who fled over-population, famine and religious oppression.

Several books containing advice to would-be immigrants were written. Some advised them how to prepare for the trip; others advised them how to get on in the new country.

ON BOARD
A 19TH CENTURY
IMMIGRANT SHIP

Imperial Oil Collection

It was the hope of a better life in British North America that sustained them on the long and terrible voyage across the Atlantic. Frequently the immigrant boats were no more than sailing vessels built to carry timber from this country to Britain. For the return voyage crude bunks were hastily constructed in the holds for the human ballast. Families huddled in misery below the decks for the trip that lasted from six to eight weeks and often longer. Their food supply, which they usually had to provide for themselves, frequently spoiled or ran short. Water supplied to them was rationed and often unfit to drink. Storms and sickness haunted the ships. For many, the dream of a new life in this country ended in a watery grave somewhere in the Atlantic.

Many of those who survived the trip and reached this province took up land. Grants of uncleared land were available from the government. For those who had some money and preferred to acquire property in an area already settled, as in Wentworth County, established farms could be purchased.

Not all, however, took to the land. Villages and towns welcomed the newcomers. Here were labourers and skilled craftsmen to help make their community prosper. A hundred and more arrived in Hamilton every week during the sailing season. Some were soon disillusioned—this was not the land of instant riches as it had been painted to them by zealous land company and shipping agents. But most found that a few years of hard work did indeed bring a better life than they could ever have hoped for in Britain.

Some worked in shops until they could acquire a business of their own. Others worked at their trade. Scottish stone masons found employment building the Burlington Canal and the Welland Canal. When these were completed many settled in Hamilton and were responsible for the numerous fine homes and public buildings of local limestone for which the city became famous.

Many, especially the Irish, found work as labourers on construction projects. Some helped with the building of the canal through the beach strip and remained to work on the wharves and in the shipyards which blossomed on the south shore of the bay. Others helped with the construction of Dundurn and received plots of land in the town as payment from MacNab. After 1850 when the railroad era arrived, it was largely Irish labour that built the local lines. Their gregarious nature led to the emergence of two of the city's most colourful areas, the "north end" around the foot of James Street and "Corktown," the area from Wellington to Catharine, south of Jackson Street to the base of the mountain.

As it had in 1832 the scourge of cholera arrived in all its fury with the immigrants of 1854. Immigrants were discharged from the ships at the Great Western Railway dock. They were not allowed into the city. Under the supervision of the health officer and the city police they were herded into sheds at the railway depot until they could be put aboard trains and sent from the area.

Hundreds of local residents fled to distant towns where the disease had not struck. But amongst those who could not leave the city, the plague took its toll. Doctors and nurses worked for days and weeks with little sleep or nourishment. Crude coffins were piled in the streets for the use of families that needed them. Again the dead carts rumbled through the streets. So swiftly and fatally did the disease strike that many died in the gutters.

Shortages occurred as farmers refused to come into the city with their produce. Many stores and businesses closed. The streets were deserted as people tried to isolate themselves from the plague. By autumn the death toll had climbed to over 500. Hamilton was reported to be the hardest hit community in the province.

Terrible as the epidemics were, a measure of good came from them. Stricter public health regulations were put into force. After 1832 resolutions were passed to ensure a better water supply and to control the operation of slaughter houses and the sale and distribution of food. Following the 1854 epidemic, a city dump was provided as a place of deposit for rubbish and refuse and dead animals from the city streets. Sewers were constructed. The building of a pumping system to bring a plentiful water supply to the city from Lake Ontario was undertaken. From such beginnings as these, the city's extensive public health services have grown.

33

In Confederation Year

Mischievously disposed people would act wisely to remember that there is a standing reward of $5 for any one who gives information against parties tearing up or removing the planks from the side-walks.

Hamilton Spectator, March 14, 1867

The cholera epidemic and the railway disaster were but memories. A royal visitor, the Prince of Wales, had spent three days in the city in 1860. During his visit he had officially opened the city waterworks on Beach Road and the Provincial Agricultural Exhibition at the Crystal Palace and had planted three elm trees on the lawn of the court house, thereafter known as Prince's Square. The city was slowly recovering from its bankruptcy of 1862 when even the furniture from city hall was sold at public auction. The din over Sir Allan MacNab's conversion to Catholicism on his deathbed in 1862 had quietened.

Members of the local 13th Battalion, Volunteer Militia, had answered the call to arms in 1866 as their grandfathers in 1812 and their fathers in 1837 had done. They proceeded to Ridgeway where they helped to clear the country of Fenians, a group of radical anti-British Irishmen living in the United States who had attempted to invade Canada by way of the Niagara Peninsula.

Fathers, then as now, turned to the pages of the *Hamilton Spectator* to read about the events of the day. The Civil War in the United States was drawing to a close. Britain, in the thirtieth year of Queen Victoria's reign, was in the midst of great industrial expansion. From Europe, the founding of the German Empire dominated the news. Overshadowing all else, however, was information about the forthcoming union of Canada West, Canada East, New Brunswick and Nova Scotia on July 1, 1867, under the leadership of John A. Macdonald.

Mothers were more concerned with the affairs of the home than they were with the affairs of the world. They read the store

138

Public Archives of Canada and Head-of-the-Lake Historical Society

CRYSTAL PALACE
This was built on the present site of Victoria Park in 1860 to house the
Provincial Agricultural Exhibition.

advertisements and market reports in the newspapers as carefully
as modern housewives check the department store and super-
market ads. Shopping was a daily affair in those days before the
invention of telephones and electric refrigeration. Farmers sold
their produce in the market behind the city hall. Huge stoves
which devoured immense quantities of cord wood dominated
every kitchen. Wood could be purchased at the John Street market
as could hay and straw by those families who had their own horse.

Such affairs, however, were of little concern to the city's school
children. They were likely more interested in being the first in
their class to own one of the erasers "of an entirely new and novel
construction" having "a gutta-percha handle, to which a small
brush is attached," as advertised in the *Spectator* on March 21,
1867, by Brown's, the booksellers and stationers on James Street.
About two months later the same shop advertised "an ingenious
and useful apparatus for protecting points of lead pencils."

A wide choice of recreational pursuits was available in the city. For sports-minded participants and spectators there was a host of activities. Cricket was still popular, especially amongst British troops stationed here, but baseball was gradually taking its place. In August, 1867, twelve local lads travelled to Detroit to take part in the world's baseball tournament. Interest in lacrosse was undergoing a revival and members of the Hamilton Lacrosse Club undertook to introduce the game to the young men of Dundas. The commencement of the annual horse racing season was enthusiastically welcomed by many. Excellent hunting and fishing were as close as the bay and marsh. One could join the Hamilton Gymnasium on James Street for an annual subscription of $3.00. The city had at least two curling rinks and three ice rinks. Skating carnivals with everyone in costume were popular events.

For those not interested in sporting activities, a variety of entertainments was offered. The Mechanics' Hall on James Street near Market Square housed such diverse attractions as minstrel shows; juggling and acrobatic performances; Hartz, the world-renowned illusionist; lectures on such topics as "an exposition

John Ross Robertson Collection,
Metropolitan Toronto Library Board

GORE PARK, 1860
Outstanding feature of the park in its early days was its ornamental fountain.

HAMILTON WATERWORKS, BUILT IN 1860
The tall chimney once served as a familiar landmark to sailors on Lake Ontario.

of the deceptive practice of professed spiritual mediums"; and plays of the day including *Oliver Twist, The Day after the Wedding* and *The Man Who Follows the Ladies.* The arrival in the city of circuses and travelling shows was well-advertised. Swingers that year were dancing something known as the galop. The soda water fountain in Hamilton's Drug Store was a popular rendezvous. For those who sought stronger drink, the city had eighty-four licensed taverns and saloons.

Those who enjoyed reading could subscribe to a wide variety of newspapers and journals. Almanacs kept local residents informed of the best remedies for what ailed them as well as the long-range weather forecast. Books could be borrowed from the library of the Mechanics' Institute. The novels of Charles Dickens and books of poetry were widely read.

Women enjoyed the inspiration and companionship offered by various church activities. Several benevolent societies existed to aid the city's less fortunate residents.

But for everyone, young or old, athletic or scholarly, the highlight of the year was the July 1st celebration of the union of British North America into one nation. The day was greeted with the pealing of bells, a barrage of firecrackers and the roar of artillery. Flags, bunting, banners and evergreen decorated public buildings and private homes. Rural folk flocked to the city to take part in the celebration.

A grand parade made its way through the downtown area and out York Street to the Crystal Palace grounds where it was reviewed by the mayor. A military display, a calithumpian parade, horse races, an Indian foot race and selections by the Great Western band added to the festivities.

In the evening buildings were illuminated, bonfires were lit along the escarpment and on King Street a magnificent fireworks display provided a fitting climax to the day's activities.

It was indeed a day and a year to be remembered!

Bibliography

Part VI (1847-1867)

Austin, P. R., "Two Mayors of Early Hamilton," *Wentworth Bygones*, III, (1962), pp. 1-9.

Canada Directory for 1857-58, Montreal, John Lovell, 1857, pp. 162-199.

Cowan, John M., "The Great Western Railway," *Wentworth Bygones*, V, (1964), pp. 2-13.

Cruikshank, E. A., *The Origin and Official History of the Thirteenth Battalion of Infantry*, Hamilton, Ruddy, 1899.

De Volpi, Charles P., *The Niagara Peninsula, A Pictorial Record*, Montreal, Dev-Sco Publications, 1966.

Guillet, Edwin, *The Great Migration*, Toronto, University of Toronto Press, 1963 (2nd edition).

Hodgins, J. George. *The Establishment of Schools and Colleges in Ontario, 1792-1910*, Vol. I, Toronto, Cameron, 1910, pp. 69-107.

O'Neil, J. G., "Chronicles of Corktown," *Wentworth Bygones*, V, (1964), pp. 28-39.

Shaw, Lillian M., "The Baker Family of Hamilton," *Wentworth Bygones*, III, (1962), pp. 30-34.

Smith, J. H., *The Central School Jubilee Re-Union, August, 1903*, Hamilton, Spectator Printing Co., 1905.

Smith, Russell D., "The Early Years of the Great Western Railway," *Ontario History*, LX, (December, 1968), pp. 205-227.

Smith's Canadian Gazetteer, Toronto, Rowsell, 1846, pp. 65-66, 75-77.

Spalding, L. T., *The History and Romance of Education (Hamilton), 1816-1950*, Hamilton, 1950.

Sutherland's City of Hamilton and County of Wentworth Directory for 1867-8, Ottawa, Hunter, Rose, 1867.

Talman, J. J., "The Newspapers of Upper Canada a Century Ago," *Canadian Historical Review*, XIX, (1938), pp. 9-23.

Part VII

. . . a manufacturing city

1873	Jolley Cut deeded to the city
1874	Queen's Plate run in Hamilton
	horsedrawn streetcars
1875	Barton Street jail
1876	*population 31,708*
1878	local telephone exchange—first in British Empire
	first bicycle in Canada brought to city by John Moodie
1881	turntable installed at King and James for streetcars
1882	City (General) Hospital
1884	cedar block paving in downtown area
	horsedrawn police patrol wagon
1886	*population 41,280*
1887	Hamilton Society for the Prevention of Cruelty to Animals
1888	Hamilton Trades and Labour Council
	cornerstone laid for new city hall on James Street North
	steamer *Macassa* begins running between Hamilton and Toronto
1890	Hamilton Public Library
1892	incline railway at James Street
1894	Hamilton, Grimsby and Beamsville Electric Railway Company
1896	*population 48,803*
	Hamilton (Central) Collegiate Institute
1897	T.H.&B. tunnel under Hunter Street
1898	hydro-electric power from Decew Falls to Hamilton
	John Moodie imports Hamilton's first horseless carriage
1899	Dundurn purchased by city

34

Made in Hamilton

Its stoves, castings, machinery, glassware, sewing machines, boots and shoes, clothing, and agricultural implements, are found in all parts of the Dominion.

High School Geography, 1887
(Canada Publishing Co., p. 74)

Skilled craftsmen making articles needed by the local inhabitants were the first manufacturers in Hamilton, as in pioneer communities everywhere. Blacksmiths hammered iron into farm implements and household utensils. Coopers fashioned barrels in many sizes for the storage and shipment of goods and produce. Wainwrights made farm wagons. Cabinetmakers handcrafted fine furniture to replace the humble, homemade furniture of earlier times. These artisans and a host of others set up shops in Hamilton and neighbouring centres. As they prospered, many were able to engage journeyman assistants to help them and an apprentice or two to whom they undertook to teach the skills of the trade.

The neighbouring communities of Dundas and Ancaster had a considerable head start over Hamilton as manufacturing centres. A wide variety of articles was produced on the water-powered machinery in the many mills beside the swiftly flowing streams passing through the villages. Hamilton, lacking good mill sites, had to wait until near mid-century when steam power came into common use. Several manufactories then appeared, intermingled with the stores and residences of the city.

The coming of the Great Western Railway hastened Hamilton's emergence as a manufacturing city. The railway made all of southwestern Ontario a potential market for articles manufactured here. Workshops and factories sprang up along the tracks near the bay front.

By the time of Confederation, Hamilton had several large manufacturing companies. The largest were the locomotive shops and rolling mill of the Great Western Railway which employed hundreds of men. A number of foundries, machine shops and boiler works kept many workers busy making machinery, castings, engines and boilers. The Gurney iron foundry, one of the largest, specialized in cast iron stoves and scales. The Sawyer company on Wellington Street North produced a steady stream of threshing machines, mowers, reapers and straw cutters. The Young brothers, manufacturers of the first coal oil lamp burners in Canada, employed a large number of hands in their brass foundry on King Street West. Three large coach factories made buggies, sleighs, cutters, coaches and omnibuses. Other firms made trimmings for these vehicles. The Wanzer company, which manufactured Canada's first sewing machine in 1860, won first prize for the best family sewing machine at the 1867 World's Exhibition held in Paris, France. Sanford, McInnes and Company employed several hundred persons to produce shoes, boots and ready-made clothing. This was the beginning of Hamilton's textile industry which gradually expanded to include spinning, weaving, dyeing, knitting and clothing factories.

Ontario Archives

THE SAWYER AGRICULTURAL IMPLEMENT FACTORY
(From *Canadian Illustrated News*, November 21, 1863)

In addition to these large firms, there was a host of smaller ones that manufactured a wide variety of articles including bellows, sails, candles, picture frames, brushes, saddles, melodeons, steel springs, spices, hoop skirt frames, biscuits, tinware, soda water, rope, locks, brooms, trunks, whips and vinegar. Most of these factories were individually or family owned. Several of them are still operating in Hamilton.

Working conditions were poor by today's standards. Most employees worked a ten-hour day, six days a week. The average wage was two dollars a day. Wages were deducted in many shops for defective work. Holidays were unheard of but much of the work was only seasonal. Buildings that had poor sanitary facilities and were poorly lit and ventilated made for unhealthy working conditions. The swiftly moving machinery was a constant threat to life and limb. Trade unions were very much in their infancy but as they grew and became more powerful, working conditions and wages gradually improved.

In the last quarter of the century Hamilton became renowned for the manufacture of glassware. The Hamilton Glass Works on Hughson Street North specialized in the making of glass containers such as fruit sealers, pickle jars and soda water bottles. The Burlington Glass Works on Burlington Street West was the most productive Canadian glass factory of its day. It turned out a wide variety of containers, tableware and lamps in a multitude of colours. Any item manufactured by either of these glass works is eagerly sought today by collectors of antique glass. Of special interest are "whimseys"—such decorative objects as canes, hats, paper weights, rolling pins, witch balls and drapes which the master glass blowers made in their spare time to practise and demonstrate their skill.

Hamilton also became the principal marketing and commercial centre for nearby agricultural communities. Its nearness to the Niagara fruit belt and good mixed farm land resulted in a large canning and food processing industry, several pickling and bottling factories, breweries, creameries, bakeries, meat packing houses and tobacco firms. A number of female employees found work in these companies.

MARKET SQUARE AT THE TURN OF THE CENTURY

The availability of cheap electric power from Decew Falls attracted many new manufacturing concerns to Hamilton in the closing years of the nineteenth century. The building of the Toronto, Hamilton and Buffalo Railway along the base of the escarpment and several spur lines to connect it with the line across the northern part of the city made available much new property suitable for small manufacturing firms.

The city council offered very attractive concessions to encourage companies to locate in Hamilton. A number of American companies were enticed to set up their Canadian branches here. Westinghouse and International Harvester were among these.

As the nineteenth century waned, Hamilton's diversified manufacturing was gradually replaced by a concentration on the iron and steel industry. The story of its growth is the subject of a later chapter.

35

The Hamilton Street Railway

A street railway train ran off the track to-day on King street. . . . A lady received a severe contusion of the — chignon, which was actually twisted out of shape by the force of the concussion, and at one time it was feared that amputation of the injured part would be necessary, but Dr. Swishtail is of the opinion that it can be saved unless mortification should unexpectedly set in.

Hamilton Spectator, May 21, 1874

By 1870 the population of Hamilton had climbed to almost 25,000 persons. The city extended from the bay shore to the foot of the mountain and from Paradise Road on the west to Wentworth Street on the east, a distance of some two and a half miles.

People of means could get around town in their horsedrawn carriages. Those who did not have their own could hire horses and buggies from the several livery stables in the city. Businessmen made frequent use of this service. So did many young men who wished to make a good impression on the young ladies they were courting. But buggies and carriages were a luxury that most people could not afford. Walking was still the most common way of getting about the city which was stretching out further and further every year. A cheap public transportation system was needed.

In 1873 a group of local businessmen received permission from the city to form a street railway company. It planned to operate "cars" pulled by horses or mules on the city streets. Six cars were purchased from a local firm and several horses were acquired (the company never resorted to using mules). Grooved rails were laid in the middle of the streets on which the cars were to run.

The first cars left the depot on Stuart Street in May, 1874. They proceeded south on James Street and then turned east on King as far as Wellington. How the heads of people on the streets must have turned as they made their initial appearance! The cars were of wooden construction with open platforms on each end. The

150

Ontario Archives

HORSEDRAWN STREETCAR
At the end of a route, the horse was hitched to the other end of the car for
the return trip.

driver sat on the open platform in summer and in winter. Bare
wooden benches ran along each side of the car. Small cars pulled
by one horse could accommodate twenty-five to thirty passengers
while larger ones pulled by two horses could hold thirty-five to
forty passengers. A maximum speed of seven miles per hour was
permitted. Passengers signalled the driver to stop by pulling a
cord suspended the length of the car.

The fare was five cents for adults and three cents for children.
It was dropped into a box on the wall at the side of the doorway.
Newspapermen, city officials and police officers were permitted
free transportation.

The company's main buildings were at Bay and Stuart Streets.
Additional barns and stables were built at convenient points
throughout the city. A handler took four or five horses from the
stable to certain intersections where these horses were exchanged
for the tired ones which were led back to the stables. The horses
were sometimes changed hourly in the heat of summer. Blacksmiths were the company's highest paid employees.

As the city expanded, the King Street line was extended eastward to Wentworth Street. It later continued along Main to
Sherman and eventually ran as far as Trolley Street (Gage Ave-

nue). Main Street East in those days was lined with large estates, each taking up a whole city block. The streetcars stopped at each house. Behind the large houses were the market farms which provided much of the city's produce.

A friendly relationship developed between the driver and his passengers. Elderly passengers were sometimes escorted to their doors by the driver. At the end of the line a kind housewife was often waiting with a cup of coffee for him. The driver stopped on request in the mornings outside a popular butcher shop on King Street near Wentworth to permit male passengers on their way to work to rush in and leave their wives' orders for delivery later in the day.

Other routes were gradually added. One ran from Queen Street along Herkimer and down James Street to the docks at the waterfront. Another ran west on King Street as far as Locke. Returning to James, it then continued westward on York as far as the Dundurn gates. The colour of the car, scarlet, green or yellow, indicated the route. Advertising on the outside of the cars contributed to company revenue. Additional routes eventually extended along Barton Street, through the west end and to Bartonville.

At the end of a route, the driver hitched the horse to the other end of the car for the return trip. At King and James where several routes met, a turntable was installed. The car was pulled onto the turntable by the horse, then the turntable was rotated until its grooves were in line with the rails on which the car was to proceed.

Large open cars pulled by two horses ran on the regular routes in the warm weather. Passengers could transfer from these cars to the steamboats at the foot of James Street for a pleasant cruise on the bay or lake. The open cars could also be chartered by a group for a special outing such as a picnic or ball game at Dundurn Park.

In winter the regular cars were removed from their wheels and placed on sleigh runners. The doorways remained open and at first only a layer of straw on the floor protected toes against frostbite. A small coal-burning stove was later added to each car.

The horsedrawn streetcars served the city for nearly twenty years. By 1892, however, the electrical age had arrived and there was a demand for more rapid transportation. The company undertook to modernize its system. A power house was built on the bay front to convert water from the bay into steam which in turn generated electrical power. The streetcars did not change much in appearance but wires overhead replaced the horses in front. The conversion took some five months and on June 29, 1892, the first "electricity cars" made their local appearance.

ELECTRIC STREETCARS
Both an open and a closed car appear in this picture. Note in the background the tower of the city hall built in 1889.

36

Home Remedies
and Learned Physicians

*Poor emigrants . . . would do well to have some powdered Ipecacuanha
with them, and should they be seized with rigors, lassitude, headache,
nausea, followed by thirst, and increased heat, they should take an
emetic of Ipecacuanha, immediately, and afterwards some laxative
medicine in conjunction with calomel or blue pill.*

Dr. Thomas Rolph, 1836
(*A Brief Account*, pp. 117-118)

There were no doctors among the first settlers who came to make
their homes in the wilderness at the Head of the Lake. These
pioneers had to depend upon their own resources in times of sickness just as they did in times of health. Some of them might have
brought with them a book of primitive remedies. Others depended
on "cures" that had been handed down in their families for
generations or passed from friend to friend. The local Indians
also instructed their white brothers in their ways of treating
injuries and diseases.

The use of native plants played an important part in these
early medications. Mrs. Simcoe was interested in the healing
properties of various plants and referred to them frequently in
her diary. When she visited this area in 1796 she recorded:

I gathered a great many plants Green gave them all names & I
stopt at his house to write them down. . . . Madder-toothach plant
a beautiful species of fern; Sore throat weed; Dragons blood—
Adam & Eve or Ivy blade very large, which heals Cuts or burns.

Shops to dispense ingredients which could not be obtained
locally soon appeared. William Lyon Mackenzie operated a drug
store in Dundas in 1820. Hamilton had three chemists by the
time it became a city.

CITY HOSPITAL,   LOCAL ADVERTISEMENT,
BARTON STREET, 1899

Many of these early remedies today seem primitive and even somewhat amusing. But these simple medicines often contained, in less refined form, many of the same elements as today's scientifically produced drugs.

Dependence on home remedies continued into the latter part of the 19th century. Most homes had an almanac which contained advice on the treatment of diverse ailments. Newspapers carried numerous advertisements for bottled "cure-alls"—various liniments, tonics and elixirs which were claimed to cure all manner of suffering. One such pain killer was recommended for no less than diphtheria, sore throat, gout, cholera, face ache, back ache, stomach ache, stiff neck, cuts, burns and frost bite. The special ingredient that many were said to contain was often only whiskey or brandy.

Doctors were usually called only as a last resort, often when it was too late to help the patient. Dr. William Case was recognized as Hamilton's first doctor. He settled here in 1810 in time to assist with the wounded at Stoney Creek. He was soon joined by several others. In those days one became a doctor by serving as an apprentice.

Pioneer doctors sometimes performed the function of dentists. A bothersome tooth was extracted with nippers and corkscrew.

Artificial teeth were uncommon and fillings unheard of. By mid-century at least one dentist had hung out his shingle in Hamilton. Two of the city's early dentists, in the absence of gas or pain-killing drugs, used to sing to their patients in an effort to distract them while the painful extraction was made.

Throughout most of the 19th century hospitals were regarded as a place where a person for whom all hope was abandoned was sent to die rather than to recover. Nursing services were almost non-existent and the patients had to tend to many of their needs themselves. Surgery was a risky undertaking with the patient more apt to die from infection after the operation than from the operation itself.

A building was erected on Aurora Street in 1848 to serve as a hospital, as well as a home for the destitute. The city animal pound and a powder magazine also shared the two-acre site. The hospital was abandoned when landslides from a quarry on the mountain side threatened to engulf the building.

The city hospital for the next thirty years was in a converted hotel at the foot of John Street. It was moved to a new building on the present Barton Street site in 1882. The site was chosen because of its quiet location well away from the noisy part of the city.

In the latter part of the nineteenth century there was a sharp increase in the occurrence of tuberculosis, then more commonly known as the white plague or consumption. This resulted in part from the growth of large industrial cities. Many people flocked to the cities seeking employment. Overcrowding, poverty and lack of sanitation, prime conditions for the spread of tuberculosis, too often resulted. Through the efforts of many dedicated citizens, Hamilton became the first municipality in Canada to possess a sanatorium for the care of tubercular patients.

Gradually techniques for the treatment and care of the sick have improved. Many doctors from this area have made significant contributions to the field of medicine. One of them, William Osler, who had to be expelled by his teachers at Dundas Public School because of his boyish pranks and misdemeanours, achieved world renown in the medical profession. After graduating from

Canadian schools, he went on to lecture at leading medical schools in the United States and England. With the rise of university medical faculties, the study of medicine was in danger of becoming a textbook and laboratory science. It was said that a student could graduate from medical school without having seen a sick person. Osler took medical students to the bedside of the sick. He was knighted in 1911 for his many outstanding contributions to his chosen field.

Hospital and medical facilities in Hamilton have steadily expanded. A significant development in the city's medical history occurred when McMaster University finally acquired its own medical school.

The city's Board of Health has also made a significant contribution to the good health of the local citizens. It has concentrated its attack on the prevention of sickness through public education and immunization programmes, reinforced by regulations and inspection when necessary. It has made great strides, in co-operation with the Board of Education, in safeguarding the health of the boys and girls of our city. Parents of Hamilton no longer live in fear of epidemics of typhoid, diphtheria, scarlet fever or even measles striking down their children.

37

Police Protection

Yesterday afternoon the handsome new patrol wagon was taken out for a trial spin. . . . The drive extended over the principal part of the city and the test included galloping at full speed on the cedar block, trotting over rough ground, going down hill with brakes on, etc. The vehicle has many advantages over the old one, its principal merit being a noiseless running gear.

Hamilton Spectator, April 9, 1889

In the first decades of settlement at the Head of the Lake, there was no police protection as we know it today. Military troops were stationed in an area in times of crisis but for the most part, settlers protected themselves and their property.

With the coming of villages and towns the practice of having a night watch was often introduced. In some communities a person was hired to carry out this function. In other communities, every able male citizen was required to take his turn at patrolling the unlit streets. At specified locations he was required to call out the time of night. Citizens in their beds were reassured on hearing the watch's call that all was well.

When Hamilton became a town, its five-member Board of Police was responsible not only for making laws affecting the community but also for seeing that these laws were obeyed and any offenders were punished. John J. Ryckman was appointed to serve as High Bailiff. He was required to arrest persons who were guilty of any breach of the town by-laws drawn up by the Board of Police and to bring such persons before one of its members. He was therefore Hamilton's first law enforcement officer. He could command any citizen to give him assistance in carrying out his duties.

Within a few years the High Bailiff was assisted by a bailiff or constable in each ward. These constables did not receive a salary. They were paid for each duty they performed such as making an arrest, escorting a prisoner or serving a summons.

158

Hamilton Police Department

BARTON STREET JAIL
It was built in 1875 of limestone removed during the construction of the
Jolley Cut.

HAMILTON'S FIRST POLICE PATROL WAGON, 1884

Eventually there were two constables in each ward. They were
required to patrol the streets every night until eleven o'clock and
until midnight on Saturdays. One of them slept at their headquarters in the engine house on King William Street. He was
responsible for ringing the town fire bell in the event of a fire.

The force gradually increased in size after mid-century. By
1855 constables received a yearly salary. Uniforms were issued.
Police station facilities were improved. A two-wheeled hand cart
with deep sides was obtained to transport drunks and other
arrested persons to the station. It was often pulled by a band of
youths anxious to assist the police. A constable could also com-
mandeer a passing wagon for conducting an unruly offender to the
station. The owner of the wagon received fifty cents for his assistance. Even wheelbarrows were used on occasion. But constables
in those days were hired for their physical strength and most of
the time they personally escorted those they arrested to the
station, carrying them on their backs if necessary.

Arrested persons were confined in cells at the police station
only until they appeared in court. Prior to the building of the
jail on Barton Street, those sent to prison were lodged at the court
house. Many were sentenced to hard labour. They were put to
work breaking up stone brought from the escarpment to the court

house square. Women prisoners were kept busy unwinding old rope which was then sold as caulking material. Any money which these labours earned was used to help pay the costs of keeping the prisoners.

In the latter part of the 19th century, the Hamilton police force continued to expand. Better methods to increase its efficiency were introduced. The force got a horsedrawn patrol wagon in 1884, the first such vehicle in Canada. The "Black Maria," as it was nicknamed, could be used to move a number of policemen quickly into an area of disturbance, round up the offenders and tote them off to the station.

About the turn of the century the department, in addition to its constables on regular patrol duties, had a squad of "fly cops" who hastened to the scene of an accident or crime—on bicycles! Constables mounted on horseback were used in some remote areas. Motorized vehicles appeared shortly before World War I and motorcycles soon thereafter. Most patrol work is now carried out in radio-equipped patrol cars except in downtown areas where policemen still walk their beats.

Like their predecessors of over a century ago, today's police constables are still only law enforcement officers. They are not law makers. Laws are made by the governing bodies elected by the people. Neither are the members of the police force responsible for the punishment of those who break these laws. Police constables fulfill their duty when they apprehend any person suspected of breaking a law and bring that person before the authorities who are responsible for determining his guilt or innocence.

But just as citizens were once comforted by the sound of the night watch's footsteps outside their windows, Hamiltonians today have security in knowing that highly trained professional police force is on round-the-clock vigilance to safeguard the life and property of every citizen in our city.

The police force of Hamilton has long had a keen interest in the young people of our city. Back in 1889, the police chief, concerned about the increase in the number of offences involving juveniles in the city, recommended that playgrounds be built for the young people of the city. The Hamilton Playgrounds Association was eventually formed and from this beginning the modern Hamilton Recreation Department has evolved.

In 1948 the Hamilton Police Minor Athletic Association took over the responsibility of operating hockey and baseball programmes for the youth of Hamilton. Hundreds of boys participate in these activities every year.

38

Access Roads and Incline Railways

. . . at last we found a way tho a very steep one to descend the Mountain.

Mrs. Simcoe's Diary, June 10, 1796

The first paths down the face of the escarpment were likely made by deer seeking water at the bay. Indians followed some of these paths and beat them into trails. One trail descended the escarpment at the head of today's John Street to connect the Mohawk trail with the one leading to the Niagara River along the base of the escarpment. Other trails made more gradual descents through the Dundas Valley and the Red Hill ravine (Mount Albion Road).

Early settlers used these same trails. The one at the head of John Street was gradually improved to permit the passage of horses and wagons. About halfway down the road stood a toll house. Those using the road had to stop there and pay a small charge. The money collected was used to keep the road in repair.

Many people who lived along the brow of the mountain and had to use the road daily objected to paying the toll. Some of them constructed crude roads down the mountain slope near their homes. Although they were not passable in all seasons, these private roads did provide a toll-free shortcut in summer and autumn for the owner and his neighbours. Such roads were built by the Horning and Filman families to the west of the John Street access. Another was built by William Strongman. Strongman's Road was useful as a shortcut but its users did not escape paying the toll as it joined the John Street Road above the toll house.

William Kerr was the owner of a fine home on the brow of the mountain at the eastern end of what is now Mountain Park. He was the fish and game inspector for this part of the province. Kerr claimed that by watching the bay through field glasses he could spot any boats engaged in illegal fishing. He had a road constructed down the mountain to make it easier for him to get to the bay shore to apprehend the guilty fishermen before they could escape. Kerr's road descended eastward from his home to join with Flock's road halfway down the slope. The road is said to have cost Kerr not much more than $100 in cash because of the help he received from neighbours.

As free public roads down the mountain came into being, these private roads were abandoned. Today all that remains of most of them are narrow overgrown pathways through the trees.

One of the shortcuts, however, did not fall into disuse. James Jolley was the owner of a saddle and harness business on John Street across from the court house. He moved to the mountain top in the 1860's at the suggestion of a physician who claimed that the fresh mountain air would be good for his wife's delicate health. He built a fine stone house at the southwest corner of today's Concession and 15th Streets.

It was not long before Jolley, who hated paying tolls, had worn a footpath down the mountain side to reach his business and his church on John Street. His path became popular with friends and neighbours. He sought permission from the city council to convert the path into a road "descending the mountain at Wellington, thence westerly along the quarries, intersecting John Street at Mr. McInnes' residence."

It took four years and nearly $3,000 of Jolley's money to chisel the road out of the limestone and shale and to grade it. Jolley then donated the finished road which still bears his name to the city on condition that the city keep it in repair and that tolls never be charged on it. He donated the limestone removed during its

162

INCLINE RAILWAY AT JAMES STREET, *c.* 1899

construction to city builders. St. Patrick's Church and the jail on Barton Street were built of limestone removed from the Jolley Cut.

In the closing years of the 19th century a novel way of going up and down the mountain was introduced. Incline railways were built at James Street in 1892 and at Wentworth Street in 1899.

Each railway consisted of two sets of tracks running side by side up the face of the escarpment. A large horizontal platform was fastened to each set of tracks. As one platform or "car" went up, the one on the other set of tracks went down. Each platform could accommodate two farm wagons and horses, several bicycles and thirty to forty passengers who sat in an enclosure to protect them from the weather. Visitors to the city were fascinated by these marvels of engineering. Many, however, would not risk a ride on them. But the inclines were very popular with mountain residents going to and from the city. They paid two cents for a trip. School children paid only a penny.

For those who wanted to save their money or for those who wanted exercise, steps were constructed beside the two incline railways and at Dundurn Street and Ferguson Avenue.

STAIRS UP THE MOUNTAIN
AT THE HEAD OF JAMES STREET
At the top is the Mountain View Hotel.
Notice the barren slopes of the escarpment.

Ontario Archives

These facilities were adequate to handle the number of people and vehicles then going up and down the mountain. But within a few decades came the automobile and a great increase in the number of people living on the mountain. Existing access facilities were soon taxed to the limit. The provision of adequate access roads became a perennial problem for the city officials.

39

New Conveniences

The District Telegraph Company have attached a new and important invention to their line. It is called the signal bell, and is singularly ingenious and useful. By its means a great number of telephones in as many different houses can be attached by one wire to a central office. . . . It is well worth inspection and will no doubt come into general use.

Hamilton Spectator, July 24, 1878

Pioneers had to depend on candles and the light from the fireplace to brighten their homes after sundown. How difficult it must have been for the boys and girls to do their school lessons in such

Bell Canada

FIRST TELEPHONE EXCHANGE IN THE BRITISH EMPIRE AT
HAMILTON, ONTARIO, JULY, 1878

dim and flickering light! Whale oil lamps came into use as people
could afford them. After the decline of the New England whaling
industry in the 1840's, however, the price of whale oil increased
and cheaper substitutes were found. Lard and camphine, a dan-
gerously explosive mixture of alcohol and turpentine, were the
common ones used.

The kerosene or coal oil lamps so avidly sought by today's
antique collectors did not come into popular use until a practical
method of refining kerosene from petroleum was discovered
several years after mid-century. The first Canadian oil refinery
was set up in Hamilton in 1860.

Although kerosene lamps and lanterns had a long and popular
life in rural areas, they were never too widely used in Hamilton.
About the time that whale oil was losing its popularity, the city
fathers explored the possibility of illuminating the whole city with
gas manufactured from coal. Lack of money prevented them from
proceeding but a group of citizens took up the idea and the
Hamilton Gas Light Company was formed. A plant to produce
the gas was built on Mulberry Street and pipes were laid.

EARLY TELEPHONES (a) 1878 (b) 1879 (c) 1880's

Bell Canada

a   b   c

By Christmas of 1850 many stores, residences and public buildings were illuminated with the yellowish light. A family could
light their home and cook with gas for fifty to seventy-five cents
a week. A month later some fifty street lamps were put into
operation. People drove into the city from miles around to see the
spectacle. The street lamps were lit half an hour after sunset and
extinguished before sunrise, except on moonlit nights when they
were not lit at all. Groups of fascinated children loved to follow
the lamplighter as he made his nightly rounds.

The telegraph quickly came into widespread use following its
first successful demonstration in the United States in 1844. Within
two years the first electric telegraph messages in Canada were
exchanged between Toronto and Hamilton.

E. Ward   Ontario Archives

A RADIAL CAR ON THE HAMILTON-DUNDAS ROUTE

ALL ABOARD THE HAMILTON AND DUNDAS RAILWAY FOR A
SUNDAY SCHOOL PICNIC, c. 1894.

Nearly thirty years later, Hugh Cossart Baker, the son of the
founder of Canada's first life insurance company, came up with
the idea of linking his home and those of two friends with a telegraph line. The three were ardent chess players and Baker thought
that they could transmit their moves in code to one another while
remaining in their own homes. The equipment worked and their
games were carried on in this fashion for two years.

They were then persuaded to try Alexander Graham Bell's
recently patented invention on their private line. After trials, a
demonstration was arranged for the press and interested persons.
The event was considered a great success as the men in the three
homes talked with one another and sang songs. The line continued
in private operation. These were the first telephones leased for use
in Canada by Mr. Bell.

Baker then formed a company to develop the invention for
public use. He visited New Haven, Connecticut, where the world's
first telephone exchange had been recently set up. He returned
to supervise the installation of the first ten telephones on his own
company's exchange. On July 15, 1878, it went into service—the
first telephone exchange in the British Empire. The local telephone directory listed 68 names by the end of the year. The first
long distance line in Canada was created in 1881 with the con-

necting of the Hamilton and Dundas exchanges. Mr. Baker's company became part of the newly formed Bell Telephone Company of Canada in the same year.

In 1884 a company was set up in Hamilton to generate electricity for public use. The electricity was generated from steam which was produced from coal. Electric lights made their appearance in city homes and on city streets.

John Patterson, a local businessman, was convinced that electrical power generated from water power was superior to and more practical than that produced from steam. He wanted to generate power at Decew Falls near St. Catharines and transmit it to Hamilton, a distance of some thirty-five miles. Experts said it could not be transmitted that far. But Patterson and a group of friends went ahead and by 1898 the generators and transmission line were in operation bringing hydro-electric power to Hamilton.

As hydro-electric power proved to be cheaper and superior to steam power, local manufacturing companies gradually converted their machinery to its use. Several new companies were attracted to Hamilton because of its abundant supply. The Hamilton Street Railway and the Hamilton Electric Company, both of which had

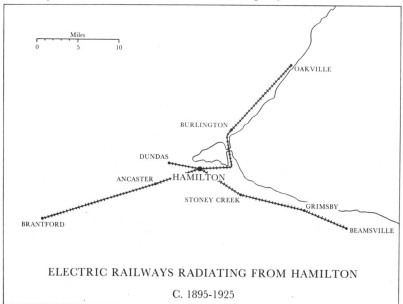

ELECTRIC RAILWAYS RADIATING FROM HAMILTON

C. 1895-1925

Hamilton Fire Department

HAMILTON FIRE DEPARTMENT, c. 1889
An efficient fire department was a necessity in the rapidly growing city.
Note the cedar blocks with which many of the main streets were then paved.

previously generated electrical power from steam, became part of
Patterson's company. It soon had a monopoly on all electrical
power in Hamilton and the surrounding area. This monopoly
continued until the company was absorbed by the Hydro Electric
Power Commission of Ontario which harnessed Niagara's mighty
potential.

The coming of electrical power also brought the electrical
railways or radials to Hamilton. Four lines radiated from Hamilton providing passenger and freight service to nearby communities.
One line ran to Dundas. Another line ran from the centre of the
city across the beach strip to Burlington and eventually to Oakville. It was well patronized by picnickers and swimmers in
summer months. The Hamilton, Grimsby and Beamsville line
was a boon to the farmers of the Niagara fruit belt. The trains
made frequent stops at crossroads along the 23-mile route to pick
up produce and bring it to the market and canning factories in
Hamilton. The last line to open ran to Ancaster and then on to
Brantford. Many students from these neighbouring communities
used the radials to commute to Hamilton to attend high school at
the Hamilton Collegiate Institute which opened in 1896.

By 1900 citizens of Hamilton indeed enjoyed many conveni-
ences undreamed of by their pioneering ancestors a century before.

40

The End of a Century

Men's navy blue flannel bathing suits, 2-piece style, with silk stitching around arm and knee, best quality, all sizes, suit . . .   *$1.25*

Eaton's Catalogue
(Spring & Summer, 1899, p. 134)

Three local newspapers, the *Spectator*, the *Times* and the *Herald*, kept people informed of the events of the day in the late 1890's. The war between Spain and the United States began and ended in 1898 with the United States acquiring Puerto Rico and the Philippines in the settlement. The world awaited news of the outcome of Robert Peary's 1898 attempt to reach the North Pole.

In 1897 Hamiltonians joined with British subjects throughout the mighty Empire to celebrate the Diamond Jubilee of Queen Victoria. Two years later several Hamiltonians joined the contingents of soldiers leaving Canada to assist Britain in the Boer War in South Africa.

But the event that most caught the attention of Hamiltonians in the closing years of the nineteenth century was the discovery of gold in the Klondike. Many men of Hamilton joined the rush to seek their fortunes in the Yukon. Most returned with exciting and harrowing tales to tell—but without any gold. Some, like Alexander Stewart, the former police chief and mayor, found only lonely graves awaiting them there.

For the thousands of Hamiltonians who could not join the rush to the Yukon there were exciting times at home. A new era opened in 1878 when young John Moodie imported the first bicycle into this country. It was a high-wheeler, commonly called a penny-farthing bicycle because of its large front wheel and small rear wheel. Such a strange contraption had a maddening effect on horses whenever Moodie took to the roads.

The bicycle with two wheels of equal size soon followed and bicycling became all the rage. Bicycles were not playthings for boys and girls as they are today. They were used for transportation and recreation by men and women who could not afford horses and buggies. Bicycle racks appeared outside stores and factories. Bicycling clubs and bicycle races became popular. The bicycle built for two was favoured for courting purposes. Women's fashions became more streamlined to permit them to ride bicycles.

John Moodie created an even greater stir in 1898 when he appeared on city streets in Hamilton's first horseless carriage. The little one-cylinder Winton manufactured in Cleveland could do twenty-five miles an hour. Mr. Winton delivered the car personally and instructed Moodie in its operation. The car cost sixteen hundred dollars. Several decades were to pass, however, before the average Hamilton family could afford such a wonder of speed and convenience.

Athletics were popular in the 1890's. The North American pastimes of baseball, basketball, football and hockey had replaced the British games popular in earlier decades. The yellow and black so long associated with teams from Hamilton was already a familiar sight. Horse racing on the track at Barton and Ottawa Streets attracted large crowds. Golf had made its local appearance. On the large lawns surrounding the homes of Hamilton's prominent families, tennis, croquet and lawn bowling were popular activities with members of both sexes.

Families enjoyed picnics and outings together. The new incline railways permitted people to scale the escarpment and spend the day rambling through woods and meadows. The radials made it possible for them to escape from the city to such far-off places as Oakville, Grimsby and Beamsville.

But the favourite playground of Hamiltonians was Burlington Bay. Landsdowne Park at the foot of Wentworth Street, Sherman's Inlet and Huckleberry Point further to the east were popular with fishermen, swimmers and picnickers. Steamers departed regularly from the foot of James Street for pleasant trips around the bay and through the canal onto the lake. Moonlight cruises with a band playing soft music were popular with young lads and maidens.

On summer weekends many families boarded the radials for a picnic at the beach. Boys dressed in sailor suits and girls dressed

Ontario Archives

AT THE BEACH AT THE TURN OF THE CENTURY
On the bay side of the beach strip looking eastward from the canal.

YACHT CLUB This elegant building stood beside the canal until it was destroyed by fire in 1915.

Head-of-the-Lake Historical Society

STEAMER, *MAZEPPA* Several steamers once plied Burlington Bay and Lake Ontario between Hamilton and Toronto.

in ruffles and pinafores helped to carry the wicker hampers containing the lunch and swim suits. Woe betide the member of the family who forgot his straw hat!

Upon arriving at the beach, they disembarked at their favourite station. Most families crossed the tracks to the bay side of the beach strip where the water was warmer than on the lake side. Father, wearing a woollen bathing suit that reached to his knees and elbows, often splashed in the water with the children. Mother usually preferred to sit on the beach doing her fancy work or reading.

After tiring of swimming, the family watched the sailboats coming and going from the gingerbread Yacht Club that stood beside the canal. The prominent citizens of Hamilton and their guests watched from the broad verandas of the club house. Many owned summer homes nearby. The swimmers and picnickers contented themselves with rowboats and canoes which could be hired from several boat liveries along the shore.

When August ended, thoughts turned again to school. Many young lads hoped that this would be the year they could abandon their Fauntleroy suits for ones of handsome Norfolk cut like those worn by the boys in the senior classes. Many girls dreamed of a soft fur muff to keep their hands warm in winter.

By late December the bay again became Hamilton's playground. Fishermen continued their pursuits through holes in the ice. Those who owned or rented a horse and cutter traversed the smooth ice while huddled under thick fur robes. Ice boats skimmed the surface at breakneck speeds. Curling had long been a familiar sight on the bay.

But of all the winter activities on the bay, ice skating was the popular favourite. Fathers, mothers and children, their blades fastened to the soles of their shoes, made their way, gracefully or otherwise, across the many miles of frozen water. Large bonfires along the shore permitted them to warm themselves. Many a hockey game took place. Some were organized and played according to the rules of the day. Most, however, were impromptu shinny affairs with anyone who was brave enough to do so, free to join in.

At home, boys and girls pored over the toy section of Eaton's and Simpson's catalogues dreaming of what they might get for Christmas. Meanwhile mothers and fathers were turning their thoughts to the new century about to dawn and what it would bring to Hamilton and the rest of the world.

Ontario Archives

CANADIAN WINTER SPORTS
(From *Canadian Illustrated News,* January 10, 1863)

Bibliography

Part VII (1868-1899)

Architectural Conservancy of Ontario, Hamilton-Niagara Branch, *Victorian Architecture in Hamilton*, Hamilton, 1967.

Blaine, Wm. E., *Ride Through the Garden of Canada, A Short History of the Hamilton, Grimsby & Beamsville Electric Railway Company*, Grimsby, 1967.

Burkholder, Mabel, "Some Eminent Citizens," *The Hamilton Centennial, 1846-1946*, pp. 77-85.

Burkholder, Mabel, "The Hamilton Street Railway, 1873-1946," unpublished manuscript, Hamilton Public Library, 1950.

Campbell, Marjorie Freeman, *Holbrook of the San*, Toronto, Ryerson, 1953.

Campbell, Marjorie Freeman, *The Hamilton General Hospital School of Nursing, 1890-1955*, Toronto, Ryerson, 1956.

Campbell, Marjorie Freeman, "70 Years With Hamilton's Street Railway," *Wentworth Bygones*, II, (1960), pp. 16-22.

Carre, William H., *Art Work on Hamilton, Canada*, 1899.

Cody, William M., "Who Were the Five Johns?" *Wentworth Bygones*, V, (1964), pp. 14-17.

Croft, F. E., "Hamilton's Marvelous Mountain," *Maclean's Magazine*, LXXII, (July 18, 1959), pp. 20-23, 43-44.

Croft, William F., "Sidelights on the Hamilton Police Force," *Wentworth Bygones*, VII, (1967), pp. 64-66.

De Volpi, Charles P., *The Niagara Peninsula, A Pictorial Record*, Montreal, Dev-Sco Publications, 1966.

Hamilton Spectator, *Summer Carnival Edition*, August, 1889.

Hamilton, The Birmingham of Canada, Hamilton, Times Printing Co., 1892.

Holbrook, J. H., "A Century of Medical Achievement," *The Hamilton Centennial, 1846-1946*, pp. 64-69.

MacNeill, Ian, "The Scamp Who Became the Great Physician," *Maclean's Magazine*, LXIV, (June 1, 1951), pp. 14-15, 36-37.

Royal Ontario Museum, *What? Why? When? How? Where? Who?* series, Toronto, University of Toronto Press.

    Brett, K. B., *Women's Costume in Ontario (1867-1907)*, 1966.

    Russell, L. S., *Lighting the Pioneer Ontario Home*, 1966.

    Stevens, Gerald, *Early Ontario Glass*, 1965.

Shaw, Lillian M., "The Baker Family of Hamilton," *Wentworth Bygones*, III, (1962), pp. 30-34.

Springer, Isabel, "A History of the Hamilton Street Railway Company," *Wentworth Bygones*, II, (1960), pp. 22-23.

Sutherland's City of Hamilton and County of Wentworth Directory for 1867-8, Ottawa, Hunter, Rose, 1867.

T. Eaton Co. Ltd., *Mail Order Catalogues*, 1884ff., on microfilm, Hamilton Public Library.

Torrance, Gordon V., *The Hamilton Police Department Past and Present, The History of Law Enforcement in Hamilton*, Hamilton, 1967.

Torrance, Gordon V., "The History of Law Enforcement in Hamilton from 1833 to 1967," *Wentworth Bygones*, VII, (1967), pp. 67-78.

Watson, J. W., "Industrial and Commercial Development," *The Hamilton Centennial, 1846-1946*, pp. 21-39.

Wentworth Historical Society, "History of the Jolley Family," *Papers and Records*, VII, (1916), pp. 9-10.

Woodhouse, T. Roy, "Hamilton—The First Telephone Exchange in the British Empire," *Wentworth Bygones*, III, (1962), pp. 24-29.

Part VIII

. . . an industrial giant

1903	91st Regiment Canadian Highlanders
1906	*population 59,543*
	opening of Mountain Sanatorium
	city's first major strike (H.S.R. employees)—Riot Act read
	Hamilton's Billy Sherring wins 26-mile marathon at Olympics in Greece
1908	first school nurse
1909	Hamilton Playgrounds Association
	Board of Control formed (mayor and four controllers)
1910	Steel Company of Canada
1912	Hamilton Alerts win football's Grey Cup
1916	*population 100,461*
1918	influenza epidemic hits city
1922	immunization against diphtheria by Board of Health
	radio station CKOC
1923	H.M.C.S. *Star*
1925	first traffic signal (at the Delta)
1926	*population 122,459*
1928	pasteurization of milk sold in the city
1929	Hamilton Municipal Airport—southeast corner of Barton and Parkdale
1930	first British Empire Games held here
	McMaster University moves to Hamilton
1936	*population 154,020*
1939	visit of King George VI and Queen Elizabeth
1940	first senior public school (Ryerson)
1942	R.H.L.I. participation in Dieppe raid

41

Steel City

To-day marks the beginning of a new era in the history and prosperity of the ambitious city, unless we are very much mistaken. To-day the fires were lighted in the furnace of the Hamilton Iron and Steel company. . . .

Hamilton Spectator, December 30, 1895

Even before Confederation, several Hamilton firms were engaged in the manufacture of iron and steel products. John Fisher built the first foundry here in 1836 and concentrated on the manufacture of farm machinery. He is credited with the making of Canada's first threshing machine. Several other foundries, machine shops and boiler works appeared. One of the largest was the Gurney company which turned out stoves, scales and machinery in its four-storey building on John Street.

The iron and steel industry came to Hamilton on a large scale when the locomotive shops and rolling mill of the Great Western Railway were set up here. In the early 1870's, however, steel replaced iron in the manufacture of rails. Its inability to compete with cheap steel from Pittsburgh's mills forced the closing of the local rolling mill.

Protective tariffs were introduced in the late 1870's to encourage the growth of the Canadian iron and steel industry which was then centred in Montreal. A group of American businessmen leased the rolling mill in Hamilton. Successful from its outset, the Ontario Rolling Mill imported scrap steel plate from England to be re-worked in Hamilton.

The building of a new Welland Canal in the 1880's was a boon to Hamilton's young metallic industry. It enabled local manufacturers to ship their products to the rapidly opening west by way of the Great Lakes. Gradually Hamilton overtook Montreal as the steel capital of Canada.

Local companies did not manufacture their own iron and steel. There had been some early attempts in Southern Ontario to smelt bog iron ore using charcoal but the pig iron produced was of poor quality. High grade pig ore could be imported more cheaply from Scotland or the United States.

In the early 1890's a Royal Commission recommended that a blast furnace for the production of pig iron be built in Canada. The city of Hamilton offered 75 acres of free land at Huckleberry Point, generous tax concessions and $75,000 for its location here.

A group of New York businessmen undertook the erection of the furnace. When it did not fare well, the company was reorganized with most of its capital raised from the sale of stock

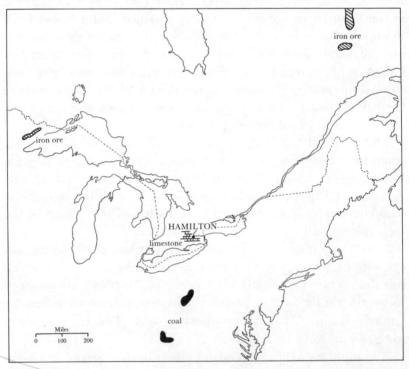

RAW MATERIALS FOR HAMILTON'S IRON AND STEEL INDUSTRY

Steel Company of Canada, Limited

Dominion Foundries and Steel

PART OF STELCO'S
BLAST FURNACE FACILITIES

STEEL BEING POURED INTO
HUGE INGOTS TO SOLIDIFY

to local people. The first iron was produced by the Hamilton
Blast Furnace Company in 1895. In 1899 it amalgamated with
the Ontario Rolling Mill and became the Hamilton Steel and
Iron Company. Open-hearth steel making was undertaken the
next year. The company expanded rapidly to become the leading
steel company in Canada.

One of the important factors in its success was the ease with
which the essential raw materials were assembled in Hamilton.
Iron ore was brought by freighter from the Lake Superior area.
Coal from the Appalachian areas of Pennsylvania and neighbouring states was imported both by ship and by train on the new
Toronto, Hamilton and Buffalo Railway opened in 1895. Limestone was readily available from nearby sources.

When American steel enterprises threatened to invade Canada
in the early years of this century, the leading steel companies of
Ontario and Montreal including the Hamilton Steel and Iron
Company united to oppose them. They merged in 1910 to become

The Hamilton Harbour Commissioners

Dominion Foundries and Steel

CENTENNIAL OVERSEAS TERMINAL BUILDING
This building, completed in 1965,
was erected on reclaimed land
at the foot of John Street.

ORE BOAT BEING UNLOADED
AT DOFASCO'S DOCKS

the Steel Company of Canada (Stelco). The head offices were established in Hamilton. The company flourished and expanded. The chief market for its output of steel was the mushrooming motor car industry.

The Dominion Foundries was founded in Hamilton by the Sherman family in 1912. It concentrated on railway rolling stock and castings for the rapidly developing mining industry of Northern Ontario. It became Dominion Foundries and Steel Limited (Dofasco) when it began to produce its own steel in 1955. It pioneered the use of oxygen in the steel-making process.

Around these iron- and steel-producing companies, there emerged a host of other companies to convert the pig iron and steel ingots into castings, forgings, plate, rolled steel, bars, rods, tubing, wire and tin plate and thence into a multitude of finished products ranging from railway cars to carpet tacks. An abundant supply of cheap electrical power, liberal tax concessions from the city, good land and water transportation facilities, a healthy climate and Hamilton's location in the heartland of Canada encouraged companies to locate here. A great influx of immigrants just before and after the turn of the century assured these companies of a plentiful supply of workers.

Essential to Hamilton's steel industry is its waterfront location on one of Canada's finest natural harbours. Vast quantities of water are used in the steel-making process. Bulk carriers can easily unload necessary raw materials at the companies' waterfront docks. Cargo ships can load finished products with equal ease for transportation to all parts of the world.

Since its formation in 1912, the Hamilton Harbour Commission has supervised waterfront land reclamation and dredging operations and the continuous expansion of warehouse and docking facilities. Activity in Hamilton's port was greatly increased with the opening of the St. Lawrence Seaway in 1959.

In 1967 some 23,000 people were employed in Hamilton's major steel companies. Thousands more worked in neighbouring factories dependent on the production of iron and steel. Since Hamilton has long been a working man's city, trade unions have played an important role in it. Through their efforts, wages and working conditions have steadily improved resulting in a good standard of living for Hamilton's factory workers.

Hamilton is often criticized as being a lunchpail town. But her thousands of factory workers are the backbone of the city's economy. The multi-million dollar income of those who carry lunchpails is the foundation on which all other commercial endeavours in the city are built. Enterprises such as stores, banks, restaurants, theatres, car dealerships and real estate agencies could not survive without the city's labour force to support them. The lunchpail carried by many of Hamilton's steel workers is a proud symbol of the city's industrial might.

42

Tiger Town

Oskee-wee-wee,
Oskee-wa-wa,
Holy Mackinaw,
Tigers, Eat 'em Raw!

Teams and individual competitors from Hamilton have brought many athletic honours to the city over the years. Some of Hamilton's athletes have won Olympic medals, the highest form of amateur athletic recognition. Many more have become members of Canadian sports halls of fame. The yellow and black colours, emblematic of numerous Hamilton teams, were adopted as early as 1874. The tiger image has been used not only in football but in hockey, lacrosse and basketball as well.

The first local athletes were the Indians. Village took on village in the ancient game of baggataway. It is still a popular sport in its modern form known as lacrosse.

Early settlers engaged in dawn-to-dusk labours had little time for athletic pursuits. But often when a group of them gathered at a tavern, a bee or even a wedding or funeral, impromptu contests of speed, strength and stamina took place. British troops stationed in this area introduced organized sports such as cricket and soccer.

In the days before automobiles, every owner was proud of his horse and many a race resulted over local roads whenever one tried to pass another. When a racing track opened on the site of Gage Park, it attracted large crowds. The Queen's Plate was run there twice. Several of Hamilton's prominent families had racing horses that brought national and international honours to their owners.

Gradually sports which were North American in origin made their appearance in this area. Hockey was first played locally on the frozen surface of the bay. One of its most popular eras was in

182

Ontario Archives

EARLY FOOTBALL MATCH BETWEEN HAMILTON AND TORONTO
(From *Canadian Illustrated News,* October 31, 1874)

the early 1920's when Hamilton had an entry in the National League.

Baseball was popular by the time of Confederation. It is said that the first playing rules for softball were drawn up in Hamilton. Played with a 16-inch ball which could not be hit far, it was a game well-suited to the vacant lots of a large city.

Hamilton's basketball teams, both men's and women's, have brought innumerable provincial and national honours to the city. As far back as 1904 a basketball team from this city participated in a tournament at the St. Louis World Fair and finished third in a field of forty.

Interest in swimming and aquatic sports has always been high in Hamilton. Its waterfront location provides excellent facilities for rowing, yachting and power boating.

The sport for which Hamilton is probably best known is football. This game dates back to 1870 when teams representing Toronto and Hamilton competed against each other. The game as then played bore little resemblance to its modern form.

In its early years members of the Hamilton Football Club paid

HAMILTON'S BILLY SHERRING
WINNING THE MARATHON AT
THE ATHENS OLYMPICS IN 1906
The king of Greece paced Sherring
for the last few yards
of the 26-mile race.

Hamilton Spectator

fifty cents annually for the privilege of playing. Total revenue for the first year of operation was $21.75. Expenses came to $20.50, leaving a profit of $1.25! The players were amateurs in the truest sense of the word. They paid their own expenses, bought their own uniforms and even carried their own lunches when the team travelled to other cities. They played only for the fun of the game. Spectator interest was keen because the players were all local lads and the fans knew many of them personally.

Another sport that has been very popular in Hamilton over the years is track and field. This local interest led to one of Hamilton's proudest moments in sport when, in August, 1930, the city hosted the first British Empire Games. Two years earlier, M. M. "Bobby" Robinson, a local sports writer and enthusiast, had been manager of Canada's track team at the Olympic Games in Amsterdam. He was so impressed with the spirit of competition and goodwill at the games that he envisaged a similar series of athletic games for competitors from the British Commonwealth and Empire countries. Because of his enthusiasm and determination, the idea became a reality.

The city officials and the citizens of Hamilton threw their support into the project. The stadium built for the Olympic trials two years earlier was enlarged to seat 16,000 spectators. The Municipal Pool was built; at that time it was the largest indoor swimming pool in Canada. Prince of Wales School was temporarily converted into accommodations for the athletes.

Five hundred athletes from ten countries gathered in the city for events in track and field, swimming, boxing, wrestling, rowing and lawn bowling. Several hundred more athletes gathered to compete for national and international honours in contests other than the official games events.

On August 16 the teams of athletes, each in its own distinctive colours, marched into the stadium. The games were officially opened by the governor-general of Canada. Canada's Olympic sprint champion, Percy Williams, took the oath on behalf of the athletes. In the week that followed, Hamiltonians had the opportunity to see many of the world's greatest athletes in action.

Athletics exist in many different forms in modern Hamilton. Community facilities such as swimming pools, tennis courts, golf courses and ski runs are used by thousands of individuals for recreation and fitness. The annual Canusa Games between Hamilton and Flint, Michigan foster international goodwill. School teams and youth teams emphasize participation and sportsmanship rather than the winning of championships. Amateur teams whose dedicated members play only for the personal satisfaction that comes from challenging competition are numerous. There are many sports which have become popular in Hamilton in recent years such as soccer, judo, rugger, field hockey, hurling, volleyball, orienteering and gymnastics. Each has its enthusiastic participants. Big-time professional sport is exemplified by the Tiger-Cat Football Club. All are a part of Hamilton's diversified sports heritage.

43

The Roaring Twenties

The Canada Ice and Coal company, limited, is putting into effect a perambulating cash and carry ice service station. . . . Delivery at the curb will be given, the customers coming to the truck and taking ice from there. . . . The regular delivery service will also be maintained for customers who wish their ice put in the refrigerator as before.

Hamilton Spectator, June 30, 1927

It was an era of peace and general prosperity, of gaiety and light-heartedness, of new inventions and comforts. It was the decade known as the "Roaring Twenties."

One of the high points of the decade was the country-wide celebration of Canada's 60 years of nationhood in the early summer of 1927. Hamilton held an Old Home Week. Local celebrations included a military pageant, music festival, air show, sacred services, parades, band concerts, fireworks and a midway. Hardball, softball, soccer, cricket, horse racing and track and field events were scheduled on the sports programme. The Confederation Jubilee Pageant at the H.A.A.A. Grounds featuring several tabloids from Canada's past earned wide acclaim.

Central School held a reunion. Among the prominent "old boys" attending was Sir John Gibson, a former lieutenant-governor of Ontario. Those who wanted to display the proper Old Home Week spirit were urged to purchase a striped tie "in the correct colours" (yellow and black, of course) for only sixty-five cents. A matching silk skull cap cost seventy-five cents.

Hamiltonians and their visitors were able to board special sightseeing buses for a tour of local places of interest including Dundurn Park, Beckett's Drive, Albion Falls, Gage Park and the east end residential section. Highlight of the tour was "the panoramic view" of the city from the top of the escarpment.

The automobile had become an accepted part of everyday life. Every family did not yet own a car but many had hopes that they

Archives, T. Eaton Co. Ltd.

Ford Motor Company of Canada

1927 MODEL "T" FORD
ROADSTER
Such a car, the forerunner of
today's sports cars and convertibles,
was the dream of many young men
in the 1920's.

FASHIONS
FOR SCHOOL GIRLS, 1927

could soon afford one. What would it be—a Reo Flying Cloud, a
McLaughlin Buick, a Whippet? What about an Essex or an Oak-
land? Or would they settle for a Ford, a Chevrolet or a Dodge?
Many young men set their sights on a flashy roadster complete
with rumble seat. In the meantime people continued to use the
streetcars, the inclines and the radials.

Great progress had been made in the air since that day in 1903
when the Wright brothers made the world's first successful airplane flight. A private flying school, the first such venture in
Canada, had been recently opened on Beach Road. Hamiltonians
followed Charles Lindbergh's non-stop solo flight from New York
to Paris in May, 1927, with interest, for Lindbergh was a direct

descendant of Robert Land. Even as Canadians prepared to celebrate their Diamond Jubilee a few weeks later, Commander Richard E. Byrd of the United States and three of his countrymen were winging their way across the Atlantic in a tri-motored monoplane.

Interest in such events was increased by on-the-spot radio coverage. A radio had become as much a part of most living-rooms as a television set was to become some thirty years later. CKOC had been on the air since 1922, but most programmes in the 1920's were the product of American broadcasting networks.

Victrolas and gramophones were popular. Hit records of the day included *Russian Lullaby* by Irving Berlin and *Honolulu Moon*. A local store urged people to buy a Jubilee recording in a "special patriotic envelope" of *O Canada, God Save the King* and *The Maple Leaf Forever*.

The granting of the right to vote to women in 1918 symbolized the beginning of a new era for Canadian women. It was the age of the flapper. Hair was short and skirts were shorter. Escorts were sportily dressed in striped blazers and white flannel trousers. The Charleston and the Fox Trot were the rage. Popular dance spots included the Alexandra on James Street South, the Arena on Barton Street, the Pier on the beach strip near the canal and the Brant Inn. Friday night dancing at the latter spot ended at 11:10 so that dancers could catch the last radial back to the city.

Motion pictures were a popular form of entertainment. Large uptown theatres such as the Pantages often presented a variety show of live vaudeville acts along with the film shows. Offerings at neighbourhood theatres during Old Home Week included *The Overland Stage*, Tom Mix in the *Great K & A Train Robbery* and Rin Tin Tin in *Hills of Kentucky*. The films had no sound tracks. Every movie house had its own pianist who provided appropriate musical accompaniment for the action on the screen. Some years were yet to pass before the Hollywood release of the first "talkie," *The Jazz Singer* starring Al Jolson.

A glance through an old newspaper of the 1920's reveals advertisements for many brands of household products which are still popular today.

Comic strips had become a feature of local newspapers. The first regular comic strip to appear in the *Spectator* was *The Gumps* in 1922. This was soon followed by *Mutt and Jeff*, *Freckles and His Friends*, *Barney Google and Spark Plug* and *Little Orphan Annie*. Other regular features included *Our Boarding House*, *Uncle Ray's Corner* and *Bedtime Story* with Uncle Wiggily.

A voyage to the "old country" cost only $170 return. A twenty-one-day, all-expenses trip to western Canada to see Banff, Lake Louise and Emerald Lake could be taken for $330. Those who could not afford such jaunts could take the boat departing for Toronto daily at 9.30 A.M. for the modest return price of seventy-five cents.

As the era gave way to the depression years of the 1930's and the war years of the 1940's, it is little wonder that people looked back with nostalgic memories on the good times of the 1920's.

44

Depression

A 17-year old mother came out of the General hospital on Monday with her first born. Unless a home can be got together for her through the generosity of citizens, she will have no home to go to. . . . The young father is out of employment and has not been able to gather anything together for the return of his wife and baby.

Hamilton Spectator, March 17, 1933

By 1929 some world economists were cautioning that the good times were over and that serious financial problems lay ahead. Trade was falling off and unemployment was mounting in Europe. Few, in United States or Canada, however, paid much attention to these warnings from Europe.

Even when news of the financial collapse of the New York stock exchange on October 29, 1929, reached Hamilton, only a small minority of its citizens were really concerned. There were some with large investments who faced financial ruin. But the average working man who had nothing invested did not think that he had suffered any financial loss. There might be a slight depression for a while but Hamilton had had depressions before. Hadn't she survived the depression of the early 1860's when the city itself had faced bankruptcy? There had been another short depression after World War I while the factories were converting their machinery to peace-time production and there were not enough jobs for the returning soldiers. By 1921, however, business had picked up. So there was little local panic in the fall of 1929 over what was happening in New York.

But the collapse of the stock market was dramatic evidence that the economic machinery of Canada and United States was no longer running smoothly. Every part of Canada felt the effects of the world-wide depression that set in.

World trade slowed to a standstill. Canada depended on trade with other countries to market her minerals, timber, wheat, fish and furs. Those Canadians engaged in the marketing of these natural products were no longer able to purchase the products of Canadian factories. This brought the depression to big industrial cities like Hamilton.

Production in local factories was cut back. Thousands were laid off. In August, 1929, Hamilton's major firms employed 40,632 workers. By May, 1933, they employed only 21,800. Many of those not laid off were put on short time. Wages were drastically cut. Meagre life savings were soon used up. By March, 1933, close to 9,000 families were receiving relief assistance. Many families lost their homes because they were not able to pay the property taxes owing on them.

The city, unable to collect taxes for municipal expenses which were increasing yearly because of the heavy relief demands, had to turn to the city banks for loans. In order to meet the city's requests, the banks had to foreclose on private loans, many of which had been made to small businesses. This, added to dwindling business and falling prices, caused the bankruptcy of many small firms and stores.

HAMILTON'S FAMOUS ROCK GARDENS
Built in an abandoned quarry, this project provided employment for a
number of men during the Depression.

The unemployed had little to occupy their time. They gathered
in parks and on street corners. They were bewildered. What was
wrong with the world that a man willing to work could not find
a job manufacturing goods which his family badly needed? Many
grew bitter. Some joined radical groups and movements.

Unmarried men were especially hard hit. They were usually the
first to be laid off and they were not eligible for relief assistance.
Many had no place to stay. To linger too long in one town or city
could result in a vagrancy charge. Many hopped the freight trains
and rode back and forth across the country looking for work.

Families practised every economy to make the dimes and nickels
and even pennies go further. People walked to save bus fare.
Bicycles appeared in great numbers again. Few thought about
fashions or new outfits. Patches even covered patches. But soap was
cheap at five bars for eighteen cents and poverty was not considered an excuse for dirtiness. Families on relief received an
average of $8.37 per person per month. Many families, not on
relief, managed on as little or less.

Housewives lived with the daily challenge of providing cheap
but nourishing meals for their families. The purchase of every
item was carefully considered. They walked many blocks to save a

penny or two on an item at another store. Advertisements read:

Oranges, dozen	21¢
Spinach, 3 lbs.	21¢
Jelly powders, each	5¢
Pork and beans, 4 tins	25¢
Pea soup, 2 tins	15¢

Bacon was 19 cents a pound and sirloin steak only 15 cents. But the average housewife could not afford even these prices for meat. Instead, she bought sausages or smoked finnan haddie for 10 cents a pound. Bread at 5 cents a loaf and potatoes at 17 cents a peck helped to fill empty stomachs.

Every member of the family did what he could to help. Young people out-hustled one another for the few part-time jobs available such as delivering for neighbourhood stores, caddying on the golf courses and picking fruit in the summer months. Many teenagers with the prospect of a steady job left school to help support their families. No job offer was refused. No one complained about working conditions.

Hard as times were, the depression years did have their positive effect. The struggle to make ends meet drew families more closely together. Neighbour helped neighbour and friend helped friend. No matter how poor a family was, there was always someone who was having an even harder time. Church groups, service organiza-

Jackson's Bakeries Limited

BREAD WAGON, EARLY 1930's   Several companies once delivered milk and bread to city homes in horsedrawn delivery wagons.

tions and the city relief department did what they could to help those who could not manage on their own. And the depression toughened people for the sacrifices demanded of them by the war years of the next decade.

The depression hit its peak in 1933. Conditions slowly improved after that. By the end of 1935 the number of families receiving relief assistance had dropped to half its record March, 1933, total. But it was not until the factories went on war-time production after 1939 that employment figures rose to the pre-depression levels. The opportunity to enlist in the armed forces attracted many young men who still had not been able to find regular employment.

Hamilton Health Association

CLASSROOM AT THE MOUNTAIN SANATORIUM, c. 1930
These young patients continue with their school work while receiving treatment for tuberculosis.

45

The Thunder of War

Our next stage was Hamilton. . . . It was the fourth of June, the grand muster day of the Provincial militia, who were assembled in some force. . . . they went through their evolutions in a manner which shewed that these citizen soldiers were not met to trifle with their duty; and that, in the event of a new war, they would prove themselves as heretofore, able defenders of their king and country.

> Six Years in the Bush, or Extracts from the
> Journal of a Settler in Upper Canada, 1832-1838
> (London, 1838, p. 12)

Conflict in Europe erupted into declared war in the summer of 1914. Posters soon appeared on poles and billboards in Canada urging young men to enlist for active service. Speakers of the Hamilton Recruiting League made nightly appeals for more manpower. Some 11,000 men and officers from Hamilton answered the call to arms.

The first group to leave the city was the 11th Field Battery. It was in action within a few months on the battlefields of France where it earned renown as the "Fighting Eleventh." It was joined by two other field batteries and two field ambulance corps from this area.

The 13th Royal Regiment of Hamilton recruited several thousand men for the battlefields of northern France and Belgium. Many went overseas with the 4th Battalion which was made up of men from several Ontario militia units. The "Mad Fourth" won ten battle honours in the trenches and mud and gas attacks of the Western Front. But the price it paid was high—four out of every five men who served with the battalion were killed or wounded.

The efforts of the 13th to get men to enlist for active service were matched by those of the 91st Highlanders. This highland regiment had been formed in Hamilton some ten years before the war with the support of the local Scottish societies. Its officers and men also served with great distinction overseas.

Hamilton became the wartime base for the Canadian Mounted Rifles. They were quartered in comfort at the Mountain View Hotel for a year until less luxurious barracks were erected on today's Scott Park site. Duties before their departure for overseas included patrolling the industrial waterfront to guard against sabotage.

When news of the signing of the armistice on November 11, 1918, reached Hamilton, its citizens let loose in joyous celebration. Whistles blew, bells rang and horns blared. People shouted, sang and danced in the streets. But they also remembered the 2,000 young men from Hamilton who did not return.

It was only twenty-one years after "the war to end all wars" that the ambitions of Adolf Hitler to dominate Europe caused Canadians to enter again into armed conflict on foreign soil. The Hamilton militia units were ordered to mobilize. Hamiltonians again responded to the call to arms. Within ten days of the declaration of war, 1500 of them had enlisted. A petrol company and a field ambulance company from this area went overseas before the end of 1939.

The Royal Hamilton Light Infantry (formerly the 13th Royal Regiment) arrived in England in time to take part in the attempted landing on the beaches of Dieppe on August 19, 1942. Hamiltonians mourned when news of this unsuccessful effort by the allies to gain a toehold on the enemy-dominated coasts of western Europe reached the city. Of the 580 officers and men of the local regiment who took part, 201 lost their lives. Many more were wounded or taken prisoner.

The regiment returned to the beaches of Normandy in July, 1944, and continued to serve in northwestern Europe. On their heels were the Argyll and Sutherland Highlanders (formerly the 91st Regiment). The 11th Field Battery also went into action in Normandy. Another field battery from this area saw action in Sicily and Italy.

Not all of the 20,000 from Hamilton who saw active service in World War II were on the battlefields, however. Many were in the skies with the 424 (Tiger) Squadron or other squadrons of the Royal Canadian Air Force. Hundreds more were on the seas in the ships of the Canadian Navy. Many young women were also in uniform performing military duties to relieve manpower for fighting at the front.

Hamiltonians again celebrated with wild abandon when World War II ended. But once more, there were the thousands of local lads who never returned.

Hamilton's contribution to two world wars was not limited to the sending of uniformed men into battle. Her steel factories were quickly converted to round-the-clock production of needed war materials such as guns, shells, tanks and airplane parts. Her textile mills turned out a seemingly endless supply of uniforms and wearing apparel. Her food processing plants helped to feed those in uniform, as well as the citizens of the war-ravaged countries. Women took the place of husbands, sons and brothers gone to war at the machines in the factories. Local church groups, service clubs and organizations spearheaded by the Red Cross packed innumerable cartons of food, knitted goods and medical supplies.

People of Hamilton, as in communities across the country, tight-

Bell Canada

VICTORY BOND FLOAT   Bell Telephone employees urge the citizens of Hamilton to buy Victory Bonds during World War I.

ened their belts and dug into their pockets. They bought victory bonds to finance the war effort. They planted victory gardens to make the food supply go further. They accepted the rationing of sugar, butter, tea, coffee and meat. The family car remained in the garage. Gasoline was rationed and new tires could not be bought. Basements, attics and garages were searched for salvage materials that could be converted into needed war materials.

Hamilton's school children gave their help. Scrap metal drives and paper collections became weekly affairs. Thousands of war savings stamps at 25 cents each were purchased every week. Ditty bags and gift parcels of such things as toothpowder, soap, chocolate and tinned goods were sent to the fighting men.

Dances and special performances were held regularly in the high schools to raise funds to contribute to the war effort. Girls knitted socks, scarves and hats. Students flocked to the district farms in the summer months to help with the harvesting. And hundreds of seventeen- and eighteen-year-olds interrupted their education to join the armed forces.

Many citizens of Hamilton continue to train in peace time with the local militia and reserve groups. They are proud to be members of military units that have earned many honours in battle. In the event of a military emergency they, like their forefathers, stand ready to serve their country. But in their hearts is the hope that this need will never again arise.

Bibliography

Part VIII (1900-1946)

Forrester, James, *Making Steel in Hamilton*, Toronto, Ginn & Company, 1967.

Hamilton, Canada, A Carnival Souvenir, Hamilton, Spectator Printing Co., 1903.

Hamilton, Canada, Its History, Commerce, Industries, Resources, Hamilton, Lister, 1913.

Hamilton Harbour Commissioners, *Port of Hamilton, 1951*, Hamilton, Davis-Lisson, 1951.

Hamilton's Jubilee of Confederation, Hamilton, W. E. Stone & Co., 1927.

Historical Records of the Argyll and Sutherland Highlanders of Canada (Princess Louise's), Hamilton, R. Duncan, 1928.

Jackson, H. M. (ed.), *The Argyll and Sutherland Highlanders of Canada (Princess Louise's) 1928-1953*, Hamilton, 1953.

Kilbourn, William, *The Elements Combined, A History of the Steel Company of Canada*, Toronto, Clarke, Irwin, 1960.

Miller, Ivan, "Champions of Sport," *The Hamilton Centennial, 1846-1946*. pp. 70-76.

Miller, Ivan (ed.), *Centennial Sports Review*, Hamilton, 1967.

Roxborough, H. H., "An Empire Olympiad," *Maclean's Magazine*, XLIII. (August 1, 1930), pp. 5, 48.

Russell, David, "A Financial History of Hamilton," B.A. thesis, McMaster University, Hamilton, 1936.

Sheehan, John, "Greatest Depression Has Sixth Birthday," *Hamilton Herald*, October 23, 1935.

Tucker, Jim, "The Comic Strip Caper," *Hamilton Spectator*, September 7, 1968, pp. 29-30.

Watson, J. W., "Industrial and Commercial Development," *The Hamilton Centennial, 1846-1946*, pp. 21-39.

Part IX

. . . . with a view
to the future

1946	*population 178,686*
1947	first parking meters
1948	Hamilton Police Minor Athletic Association
1950	Tiger-Cat Football Club
1951	trolley buses replace streetcars
	visit of Princess Elizabeth and Prince Philip
1954	CHCH-TV
1955	Greater Hamilton Shopping Centre
1956	*population 225,638*
	one-way street system
1958	completion of Burlington Skyway
	first Canusa Games between Hamilton and Flint, Michigan
	women police constables
1959	nuclear reactor opened at McMaster University
1960	city's boundary extended to south of Highway 53 (Rymal Road)
	Chedoke General and Children's Hospital
	last horsedrawn milk wagon
	opening of new city hall (Hamilton's fourth)
1962	Woodward Avenue sewage treatment plant
	Memorial Cup win in hockey for Hamilton Redwings
1964	Chedoke Winter Sports Park
	Confederation Park
1966	*population 283,099*
	Terminal Towers
1967	restoration of Dundurn Castle

46

Newcomers

... the poorest individual, if he acts prudently and is industrious, and has a common share of good fortune, will be able to acquire an independence in the space of four or five years.

John Howison, 1821
(*Sketches of Upper Canada*, p. 238)

At some time in the history of every Hamilton family there occurred an emigration from another country. In some families it happened several generations ago. In others it might have taken place within the past few months.

Even the forefathers of those of Indian blood came to this area from elsewhere. The story of the annihilation of the Neutral nation which once inhabited this area has already been told. Nomadic Algonkian tribes and members of the Six Nations Confederacy from south of Lake Ontario later moved into these parts.

Then came the first white settlers, the United Empire Loyalists, to build new homes for themselves in the wilderness at the Head of the Lake. Many were of British ancestry; many were not. Thus from its very beginning Hamilton was populated by people of diverse origins.

The Loyalists were followed by others from the United States. Many were opportunists attracted by offers of free land. They too contributed their ambitions and skills to Hamilton's growth. After the War of 1812, however, Yankee immigrants were no longer very welcome in Upper Canada.

The next several decades brought a great number of settlers from England, Scotland and Ireland. Their contribution to Hamilton's development in the mid-1800's has been described in an earlier chapter.

Several Negroes who had been slaves in the southern states and had run away from their owners made their way to Hamilton in the mid-nineteenth century. As early as 1843 the coloured people of Hamilton requested and were granted equal educational opportunities for their children.

In the latter part of the nineteenth century, hundreds of thousands of immigrants from continental Europe joined the continuing stream from Great Britain. Forsaking their homelands because of religious oppression, political strife, overpopulation or economic instability, they hoped for a better life in Canada. Many, especially from eastern Europe, headed for the Canadian west where they took up land. Others were attracted to the growing industrial cities of eastern Canada. Skilled or unskilled, they became part of the labour force needed on the construction projects and in the factories of cities like Hamilton.

They were joined by a number of American businessmen with an eye to the profits to be made by expansion into Canadian markets. Fledgling companies welcomed their ideas and managerial experience.

The influx of immigrants continued into the early years of the twentieth century and reached its peak in 1913. After being interrupted by World War I, it resumed in the 1920's. However, during the depression and World War II years, it slowed to only a trickle.

Hamilton's population was swelled by more than 50,000 immigrants in the fifteen years following the end of World War II. Among the first to arrive were the European brides of returning servicemen. They were followed by a great number of displaced persons who, uprooted by the war, were unable or unwilling to return to their homelands. Many fled the Communist web that settled over much of eastern Europe. Thousands more chose to leave their crowded homelands in western and southern Europe to make new opportunities for themselves and their families in Canada.

A large number chose the Hamilton area because they had relatives already living here. Some, especially those from the Netherlands and eastern Europe, went to work on local farms. Many found work on the numerous construction projects in the rapidly growing city. Others were needed in Hamilton's constantly expanding factories and steel mills. A high percentage were skilled craftsmen and technicians who contributed their knowledge and experience to Hamilton's postwar development. Women immigrants found employment in the city's textile mills and food processing plants. Among the newcomers were professionally trained people who soon took up important roles in education, medicine, research, industry and government.

Many of those who immigrated to this area have since acquired their own businesses. They have become the proud owners of farms, stores, restaurants, manufacturing concerns, construction companies and a host of other endeavours which in turn create additional jobs on the local labour scene.

The newcomers' talents and cultural backgrounds have helped to foster interest in Hamilton in opera, music, ballet, theatre, painting, sculpture, architecture and handicrafts. Various ethnic groups have been responsible for popularizing judo, gymnastics, soccer, field hockey, volleyball and many other sports on the city's athletic scene. Foods such as spaghetti, cabbage rolls and chicken chow mein have become as much a part of the local diet as hamburgers. The postwar newcomers have contributed towards an enriched life for all Hamiltonians.

HAMILTON'S PEOPLE (1961)

STATUE OUTSIDE
EDUCATION CENTRE

Population, 1961	273,991
Born in Canada	188,253
Born outside Canada	85,738
Immigrated 1946-61	50,410
Ethnic group	
British Isles	161,350
French	11,493
German	14,171
Italian	23,203
Netherlands	6,910
Polish	11,412
Russian	1,354
Scandinavian	2,210
Ukrainian	8,559
Other European	23,954
Asiatic	2,069
Other and not stated	7,306

SOURCE: Dominion Bureau of Statistics, Eleventh Census, 1961, *Bulletin CT-8, Hamilton*, p. 4.

47

City Planning and Urban Renewal

The streets of Hamilton are generally laid out at right angles; those running back from the Bay having a direction nearly north and south, and being crossed by others running east and west.

The Canadian Directory for 1857-58 (p. 162)

As Augustus Jones trudged with surveyor's chain and blazing axe over the land at the Head of the Lake dividing it into one-hundred-acre lots, who could then foresee that he was establishing the skeletal form of one of Canada's leading cities? His concession road allowances eventually became Hamilton's east-west arteries. The side roads became its principal north-south streets.

Following the example of George Hamilton, neighbouring farmers gradually sold off their property. Land along the concession roads and side roads was generally sold first, often for commercial purposes. The rest of the farm was eventually subdivided into residential streets and building lots.

Hamilton's distinctive topographical features influenced and controlled the pattern of the city's development. The municipal institutions and commercial enterprises such as stores, banks and business offices were built on the Iroquois plain. Fine residential areas, parks, recreational facilities and some light industry appeared to the east and west of the downtown core. Heavy industry sought the cheaper land close to the bay front. Inlets and marshy areas were easily filled to become ideal factory sites. Most of the main rail and road facilities were funnelled into the city by way of the high and low level bars. Thus Hamilton was spared during its formative years from the blight of many North American cities which tended to grow outward from the centre in a hodgepodge of residential, commercial and industrial activity. Hamilton was able to develop its industrial potential without sacrificing the beauty of its setting.

However, even in a city like Hamilton where land use was initially controlled by topography, growth and development can

204

no longer be left to chance. Zoning by-laws are a necessity in a modern city. The city planning department ensures adherence to these by-laws and oversees long-range land use planning.

The escarpment was once considered a natural barrier to the city's southward expansion. But the automobile has surmounted this obstacle. Development on top of the escarpment since the end of World War II has been phenomenal. It is predominately a residential area with controlled commercial activity and very little industry. The opportunities for expansion, which is rapidly engulfing the seventh and eighth concessions, are virtually unlimited.

The demand continues for more housing to fulfill the needs of the growing population. Housing surveys in the past were too often characterized by series of parallel streets, each lined with a double row of stereotyped houses. Modern developers attempt to avoid such drabness by building homes of varying designs on

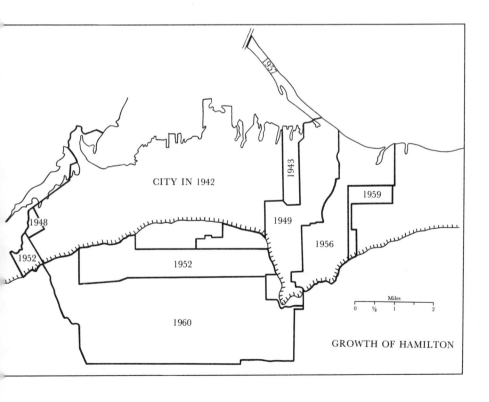

CITY IN 1942

1937

1943

1948

1952

1949

1952

1959

1956

1960

Miles

0   ½   1   2

GROWTH OF HAMILTON

short streets, courts and crescents. As land costs climb higher, condominium housing and high-rise apartments dominate more and more of the urban scene.

Open spaces and recreational facilities are carefully integrated into the overall design of a neighbourhood. Schools are no longer factory-like structures located on heavily travelled main streets. They are nestled, where possible, in the midst of surveys and are designed to compliment the architecture of the surrounding homes. Stores and services, instead of being spread out along the main arteries, are clustered into neighbourhood malls and plazas with ample parking facilities.

The regulation of vehicular traffic becomes a serious problem in downtown areas as cities grow larger. People come to rely more and more on public transportation systems to take them into and out of the city centre. Hamilton, some experts say, cannot provide such facilities, as many other cities have, by tunnelling beneath the city. It is claimed that the sedimentary nature of Hamilton's substrata will not support an underground subway system. Hamilton could become a pacesetter in the development of an imaginative surface or above-surface rapid transit system.

Expressways to facilitate the flow of traffic around and through the city have become a necessity. Hamilton also has the special problem of providing adequate access facilities between the lower and upper city. Careful planning is needed for these multi-million dollar undertakings.

CONDOMINIUM HOUSING
As land costs rise, more and
more of this type
of housing appears.

CONSTRUCTION OF A
HIGH-RISE APARTMENT
The number of these
towering structures increases every year.

Older sections of a city gradually deteriorate. Buildings erected over a century ago fail to fulfill modern purposes. Several urban renewal projects have been undertaken in Hamilton.

The first section of the city to receive extensive rehabilitation was the once-attractive north end residential area below the C.N.R. tracks, westward from Wellington Street. Many homes received complete renovation. Others were razed to make way for parks, new schools, perimeter roads, a community centre, a shopping area, public housing and a senior citizens' apartment. From the experience learned there, several other urban renewal projects were planned.

The most ambitious of all was the Civic Square project with the new city hall, opened in 1960, as its southern focal point. Shabby buildings and parking lots were cleared to make way for a new library, art gallery, theatre-auditorium, hotels, office towers and shopping malls co-ordinated with broad open areas and promenades. The first tangible evidence of this undertaking to revitalize the downtown core of the city was the completion of the Education Centre in 1967.

Early communities on this continent had village squares where the people could meet and communicate with one another. The civic officials of Hamilton have shown insight in trying to recapture this concept. The Civic Square is meant to be a place where the citizens congregate to take an active part in communal activity.

48

Conservation and Pollution Control

. . . is it not absolutely necessary that the inhabitants should have some places to breathe the pure air, in their hours of recreation, without being blinded in the dusty streets, or cooped up night and day in their houses?

Hamilton Spectator, July 24, 1847

Hamilton has been blessed with a rich natural heritage. In past decades this heritage was generally taken for granted. Often it was pillaged and desecrated.

The wholesale clearing of tree-covered plains and valleys began with the first white settlers. Primeval forests gave way to farms which in turn gave way to housing surveys.

The escarpment was regarded by many people as a nuisance— an obstacle between the plain below and the plateau above. Quarrying operations hacked into its limestone rim. Brick yards gouged out the clay at its base. Roads were blasted along its face. Picturesque ravines became garbage dumps.

Less than a century ago, Burlington Bay was Hamilton's playground. But it became a convenient dumping place for the city's raw sewage. Factories sprang up on its shores. Untreated industrial wastes and chemicals were discharged into its waters. Hamiltonians were inclined to accept the resultant pollution as part of the price they had to pay for progress.

The air over the city grew dirtier as more and more chimneys belched their fumes into the air. Factories were not the only culprits. Stores, schools, apartments and houses contributed to the growing problem of air pollution. Automobile exhaust systems added their poisonous fumes to the atmosphere. Again the majority of the people of Hamilton accepted the smog as an inevitable part of life in a large industrial city.

But gradually people have begun to realize that such conditions and practices are a threat to their well-being. Open dumps are an

208

ICE CUTTING ON HAMILTON HARBOUR   Ontario Archives
Ice was cut in large chunks and stored in ice houses along the bay shore to
await summer delivery to city homes. Pollution and electric refrigeration
put an end to this activity in the 1920's.

eyesore and a breeding place for vermin. Trees in the environment produce life-giving oxygen. They retain moisture in the
soil to prevent excessive spring run-off followed by summer
drought. The polluted waters of the bay drain into Lake Ontario
from which the city obtains its water supply. Smog-laden air is
injurious to health. Even the rising noise level in the city, some
medical experts warn, has a damaging effect on hearing and
mental health.

Green acres within a city provide recreational facilities for
people seeking relaxation from the quickening pace of everyday
living. The Hamilton Parks Board has been providing such areas
and facilities for the people of Hamilton since its formation at the
turn of the century. The development of Chedoke Winter Sports
Park, Confederation Park and King's Forest are ventures to help
meet the recreational needs of a modern city.

After years of abusing the escarpment, citizens and civic officials
of Hamilton came to realize that it was one of the city's most distinctive features and worthy of better preservation. The city
purchased the property along the face of the escarpment from
Chedoke Falls to the Albion ravine in 1913. Thousands of trees
were planted to cover the scars of the past. A man was hired to
protect the trees which gradually grew to form a green backdrop
to the lower city.

To countless numbers of local boys and girls the escarpment has served as a wilderness stage. A touch of imagination easily transformed it into Sherwood Forest, Mount Everest, the Amazon jungles or the surface of the moon. "Indian trails" and secret hideaways have long abounded on its slopes. In the past thousands of Hamiltonians took part in the annual Good Friday hike up the train tracks to Albion Falls. Today's hikers can traverse the city on the Bruce Trail that follows the escarpment from Queenston to the tip of the Bruce Peninsula. Many conservationists envisage the day when the escarpment, along its entire length, will be made a national or provincial park.

Hamilton's world-famous Royal Botanical Gardens date from 1930. An early venture was the transformation of some abandoned gravel pits on the high level bar into the magnificent Rock Gardens. This was followed by the development of the impressive western entrance into the city by way of the same bar.

Today, in addition to its extensive horticultural display areas, the property of the Royal Botanical Gardens includes several hundred acres of land around Cootes Paradise and in the lower Dundas Valley which are maintained in their natural state. Miles of trails wind through these sanctuary areas. The Gardens' staff

A YOUNG HIKER ON THE BRUCE TRAIL
The trail is marked with blazes of white paint, six inches long and two inches wide.

MAPLE SYRUP DEMONSTRATION AT ROCK CHAPEL
This activity, sponsored by the Royal Botanical Gardens, attracts thousands of visitors every March.

and supporters conduct an active nature interpretation programme in which young people are encouraged to participate. Thousands of people attend the yearly demonstration of maple syrup making at the Rock Chapel Sanctuary.

Through sound conservation practices, the recently formed Hamilton Region Conservation Authority attempts to preserve the natural resources of the Hamilton area and provide outdoor recreational facilties for local residents. Its initial efforts were mostly in the Spencer Creek watershed but have since expanded to encompass other areas.

Steps are being taken to halt the pollution of Hamilton Harbour. The building of a modern sewage treatment plant stopped the pouring of tons of raw sewage into it. Industries have been required to control the dumping of wastes and chemicals. Although the cost would be very high, it is said that the water of Hamilton Harbour could be improved to a degree that fishing and even swimming could again take place there.

It has been proven in other large industrial cities that smog can be controlled. The civic and provincial governments have introduced measures to lessen the problem in Hamilton. Local industries have spent large sums of money to instal equipment to combat air pollution.

But the problem of pollution cannot be solved by government and industry alone. People also cause pollution. An ashtray emptied onto a parking lot, a gum wrapper dropped onto a city street, a pop can tossed away under a bush in a city park . . . large sums of public money have to be spent annually to clean up such litter. Every citizen has a stake in the fight against pollution for a polluted environment is both unsightly and unhealthy.

49

Recreation

*I got up early this morning to work in my garden, and after breakfast
I went down to it again . . . . Minnie and I had just finished making
a path when we were called in . . . . I amused my self copying some
sacred music and writing my journal.*

Sophia MacNab's Diary, May 4, 1846

The early settlers in this area worked from dawn to dusk to provide shelter and food for their families. They had little time for
recreation. They were able to get together for an occasional bee
but even then their hands were busy with such tasks as making
quilts, paring apples, threshing grain or chopping firewood for
the long winter months ahead.

Just a hundred years ago most people worked ten hours a day,
six days a week. The seventh day was the Sabbath, the day of
worship. Vacations for workers were unheard of. Yet somehow,
people still found time to visit with their families and friends,
play sports, go fishing, do fancy work, join literary groups, belong
to benevolent societies and the like.

Today most Hamiltonians work a forty- or thirty-five-hour week.
They fill the remaining hours with a wide variety of recreational
activities. Some find their greatest satisfaction in their leisure
hours in being together with their families and friends. Some
enjoy puttering around their homes; they find pleasure in decorat-
ing, remodelling or gardening.

Many seek recreational pursuits outside their homes. No matter
what a person's hobby is, he or she is certain to find in Hamilton
a club or a group of people with a similar interest. The Hamilton
Recreation Department plans programmes for all age groups at its
neighbourhood community centres. City parks are intended for
use by the people of the city. Facilties including swimming pools,
skating rinks, golf courses, ski runs, playing fields, tennis courts
and stadiums. The athletically inclined can choose from the multi-

tude of individual and team sports played in the city. Organizations such as the Y.M.C.A., the Y.W.C.A., the Jewish Community Centre, the Germania Club and the Catholic Youth Organization provide a variety of physical, cultural and social activities.

As Hamilton grows, it becomes noisier. Everyday life becomes increasingly more hectic. Many people seek relaxation and peace of mind in their leisure hours. Some find these in such outdoor activities as strolling along a wooded path, picnicking in a quiet glen, listening to the springtime chorus of the returning birds or watching a majestic sunset. Hamilton has a well-endowed natural environment where these pastimes can be followed. There is the wooded face of the escarpment. There are the nature sanctuaries of the Royal Botanical Gardens. There are the conservation areas developed by the Hamilton Region Conservation Authority. Several local clubs and associations foster outdoor recreation.

Others seek stimulation through what might be called cultural pursuits. Adequate libraries, museums and art galleries are an important part of the modern urban scene. For too long, Hamilton was without satisfactory facilities for those who wished to

HAMILTON PHILHARMONIC YOUTH ORCHESTRA
These young musicians practise diligently under the baton of Glenn Mallory.

Hamilton Spectator

Hamilton Spectator

CHEDOKE WINTER SPORTS PARK
Excellent skiing facilities exist within the city limits on the slopes of the escarpment.

THE COCKPIT THEATRE
Restored by the *Spectator* as its Centennial project, MacNab's cockpit serves as a stage for children's plays in the summer months.

enjoy a musical concert, a theatrical presentation or a ballet performance. Local groups such as the Hamilton Theatre Company, the Players' Guild and the Hamilton Philharmonic Youth Orchestra provide opportunities for those who want to participate actively in such endeavours.

Night school has become a way of life for thousands of Hamiltonians. While many take courses to improve their employment opportunities, many more attend for the pleasure that comes from such achievements as painting a picture, building a hi-fi set, reupholstering a chair or learning to speak a foreign language.

Many people continue to find fellowship and satisfaction from belonging to church organizations and service clubs. Some enjoy the challenge of a cause whether it be raising funds for a new church organ, supplying braces for crippled children or spearheading the preservation of a fine old building. Hundreds of

Hamiltonians spend many hours of their leisure time as leaders of the numerous youth groups in the city.

Many economists say that in the not-too-distant future the average worker will work considerably fewer hours than he does today. Many, it is said, will never work at all. Such predictions raise many interesting considerations. Throughout history human beings have had to work if they and their families were to survive. Will people be able to adapt to a life consisting mostly of leisure time? Will they be able to fill their non-working hours with satisfying activity? Will they be able to keep their bodies in good physical condition and their minds active and alert through stimulating interests and pursuits?

50

Education for All

... I want to take this opportunity of expressing the interest I feel in the Central school. In it I learned lessons, and had my ambition stirred up, due to the sincere, earnest and inspiring way in which the principal discussed with pupils what they might become.

Sir John Gibson, 1927 Central Reunion
(*Hamilton Spectator*, June 30, 1927)

With the Central School as its cornerstone, the public educational system of Hamilton expanded steadily. By 1887 the city was divided into five school districts. Each district had one leading school and one or more primary schools. The leading schools were Queen Victoria, Central, Hess, Cannon and Victoria Avenue. The headmaster of the leading school was in charge of all the schools in his district.

Birch rods were abolished in 1872. Field days or sports days came into being ten years later. Kindergartens made their appearance in 1885. An exhibit of school work by Hamilton school children was shown at the Chicago World's Fair in 1893 and received special commendation in the form of a diploma. Nominal school fees were still being charged at the turn of the century—10 cents a month for primary children and 20 cents a month for other pupils. After years of effort by the Local Council of Women, household science (home economics) and manual training (shop) became part of the curriculum early in the new century. The first school nurse was appointed in 1908. Special classes for the handicapped and disadvantaged were begun two years later.

The number of elementary schools steadily increased in the latter part of the nineteenth century and the first three decades of the twentieth century as new areas of the city were developed. Several schools were acquired through annexation. The system of having leading and primary schools was replaced by that of having Junior 1st (Grade One) to Senior 4th (Grade Eight) in one school, each under the direction of its own principal.

216

MOHAWK TRAIL SCHOOL MUSEUM
These students are finding what schools were like in great-grandfather's day.

No new elementary schools were built during the depression years of the 1930's or the war years of the 1940's. Two significant developments in the elementary school system during this period were the introduction of the unit system of promotion and the opening of the city's first senior public school (Ryerson).

Secondary education was removed from the Central School to a new grammar school at the corner of Main and Caroline in 1866. Thirty years later it was again moved to larger quarters with the opening of the Hamilton Collegiate Institute on Hunter Street just west of Victoria Avenue. The raising of the school-leaving age to sixteen after World War I resulted in more and more young people attending high school. The Hamilton Technical Institute on Wentworth Street North opened its doors in 1919, followed by Delta, Westdale and the Central High School of Commerce within the next few years.

The growth of the city's educational facilities since the end of World War II has been phenomenal. In 1945 there were thirty-two elementary schools. Twenty years later there were seventy-five. Enrolment more than doubled during this period. By 1967 there were twelve secondary schools and four special vocational schools.

The city's separate school system has also grown steadily. St. Patrick's and St. Mary's opened the year following the passing of the Ontario Separate Schools Act in 1855. By 1967 there were thirty separate schools.

Young people are staying at school longer than ever before. Before 1900 an elementary school education was considered good enough for one to work on a farm or in a factory. In the first half of this century, a secondary school education was adequate preparation for most jobs. But young people of today know that more and more types of employment require some form of post-secondary education.

Hamilton became a university city in 1930 when McMaster moved from Toronto to forty-eight acres of Westdale park land. A local fund drive raised over half a million dollars towards its establishment here. It has since expanded to many times its original size. McMaster students today have a wide choice of courses in many fields including the arts, humanities, sciences, business, engineering, theology and medicine.

Mohawk College of Applied Arts and Technology offers extensive opportunities for those who want higher education of a practical, rather than of a professional or literary nature. A wide range of technical and technological courses is available to high school graduates. Courses in business and in applied arts are also offered.

As society changes, so do the aims and objectives of education. In pioneer times schools were considered to be fulfilling their function if they taught students the basic fundamentals of reading, 'riting and 'rithmetic. As more and more people in this part of the country became urban dwellers, emphasis in schools was placed on the memorizing of facts and the acquiring of skills so that young people could take their place in the working world.

But in the ever-changing technological world of today, skills often become obsolete before they can be put to use. On-the-job training and retraining are becoming a part of every job. Continuous learning is becoming a part of every worker's life. The challenge facing today's educators is to develop in young people the desire and ability to discover and learn for themselves.

As the average working week is shortened, modern educators also realize a responsibility in motivating young people to use their abundant leisure time for the betterment of both themselves and the society in which they live.

A VISIT TO THE FARM FOR A GROUP OF PRIMARY PUPILS

51

Centennial City

The birthday of our new Dominion will long be remembered in Hamilton, and we trust many happy returns of the day will be celebrated with equal loyalty and patriotism.

Hamilton Spectator, July 2, 1867

If a local celebrant of Canada's birthday in 1867 were to return to Hamilton a hundred years later, would he recognize the city he once knew? He might identify a few vaguely familiar landmarks—the enduring escarpment, the bay, Gore Park, the old engine house on King William Street, the Central School, St. Paul's Church, the stone customs house on Stuart Street, the 1860 pump house near the lake. His mind would undoubtedly reel, however, at the sight of the throngs of people, the streams of cars and trucks and buses, the bewildering store displays, the towering buildings of glass and concrete and the huge factories hugging the bay shore.

But he would find the Hamiltonians of 1967 celebrating Canada's centennial with as much enthusiasm and fervour as his compatriots celebrated its birth a century earlier.

One of the city's first steps to prepare for the gala year was the choosing of William McCulloch to be the local centennial chairman. He threw himself into the task with the same energy with which he had been organizing local community efforts for over thirty years. He was an avid local historian and a gifted speaker who could arouse in people an excitement for any undertaking. A multitude of plans for the local celebration of Canada's hundredth birthday soon took shape.

Some four hundred people gathered in Gore Park on New Year's Eve to watch Mayor Victor Copps, in gay party hat, light the symbolic green maple leaf to usher in centennial year. Ahead were 365 days of special events and celebrations.

The city's centennial project was the restoration of Dundurn

Castle to its beauty and function of 1855. Many months of detailed research and meticulous workmanship culminated in the official opening of the castle on June 17. On hand for the occasion was the current chieftain of the MacNab clan who brought with him a letter written by Sir Allan 108 years before inviting his chieftain to visit Dundurn.

On the evening of June 30 thousands gathered in Gage Park for a mass military and sacred service. Few Hamiltonians went to bed until after the midnight firing of one hundred rockets from the brow of the escarpment to herald Canada's official birthday.

Thousands thronged the downtown streets the next morning to view the big parade. The local militia units and veterans led off. Then came Mayor Copps and his family, appropriately attired and riding in an antique car. Several bands, dozens of floats and hundreds of marchers and performers passed by. Hamiltonians of 1967 showed they loved a parade as much as their forefathers of a century before.

HAMILTON'S CENTENNIAL
PARADE, JULY 1, 1967

A UNIQUE CENTENNIAL PROJECT
M. Fortney displays his detailed scale model of downtown Hamilton in 1867.

Practically every local club and organization undertook a special centennial project. There were displays, concerts, dances, reunions, contests, speakers, donations, dinners and publications. Regular events such as the Canusa Games received special emphasis in centennial year. Practically every citizen had his or her own personal project. The projects ranged from the beautiful to the bizarre. But all were a manifestation of the excitement and enthusiasm of 1967.

Never was the human wealth of the city more vividly displayed. Each ethnic group was allotted one week in which to display, for the enrichment and enjoyment of the citizens of Hamilton, its cultural heritage and its contributions to our city.

The city's separate schools co-operated to stage a historical pageant made up of excerpts from Canada's history. Eight performances were held at the Mountain Arena.

Every Hamilton public school was encouraged to initiate its own projects. Pupils visited other schools, made collections, reenacted historical events, dressed in period costumes, made scrapbooks, wrote stories, poems and plays, had special visitors, planted trees, took trips and excursions, sketched and painted, sang and danced . . . and in doing so, they learned about their great country—its past, its present and its future.

The Hamilton Teachers' Council and the Board of Education with assistance from the local Home and School Council restored Mohawk Trail School. Hundreds of thousands of Canadians once attended one-room schools similar to this one built in 1882. It was therefore decided that such a school was worthy of preservation so that boys and girls could see for themselves what schools of bygone days were like.

There were several special events which, although not centennial projects, added excitement to the local scene in 1967. A public campaign to raise funds for the long-awaited civic auditorium was launched. Federal government approval was given to the Civic Square concept. The Education Centre was opened. Plans for a Gore Park facelifting and the development of King's Forest were announced. Governor-General Michener came to the city for the installation of the first president of Mohawk College. Thousands of children were immunized in a one-day blitz against measles. The Tiger-Cats won the Grey Cup.

Most thrilling of all was the Miles for Millions march in November when some 17,000 persons, most of them high schoolers, undertook to raise money in aid of several African projects. Sponsors agreed to pay the individual participants for every mile walked. More than half of the walkers, Mayor Copps amongst them, completed the entire thirty-five-mile route. Over $175,000 was collected. Never were the grown-ups of Hamilton more proud of the young people of our city.

All too soon, centennial year drew to a close. As a fitting climax, Bill McCulloch, the man who had made things happen, was named Hamilton's Citizen of the Year and the recipient of the first Hamilton Medal ever awarded.

It was a year of fun and festivity. It was a year for looking back over a proud past. Even more, it was a year for looking ahead to an exciting future.

MILES FOR MILLIONS. 1967

Bibliography

Part IX (1946 ff.)

Bastin, E. W., "A City that Cares," *Canadian Audubon*, XXI, (September-October, 1959), pp. 110-114.

Beattie, Jessie L., *John Christie Holland*, Toronto, Ryerson, 1956.

Beattie, Jessie L., *Strength for the Bridge*, Toronto, McClelland & Stewart, 1966.

Burkholder, Mabel, "Hamilton Prideful Over 1889 School Facilities," *Hamilton Spectator*, January 28, 1961.

Cockman, William, "Hamilton's Royal Botanical Gardens," *Canadian Geographical Journal*, L, (June, 1955), pp. 228-236.

Croft, Frank, "Hamilton's Marvelous Mountain," *Maclean's Magazine*, LXXII, (July 18, 1959), pp. 20-23, 43-44.

Croft, Frank, "Streets of Canada: James," *Maclean's Magazine*, LXXII, (October 24, 1959), pp. 24-25, 95, 100.

Dominion Bureau of Statistics, Eleventh Census, 1961, *Bulletin CT-8, Hamilton*.

Dominion Bureau of Statistics, *Canada One Hundred 1867-1967*, Ottawa, Queen's Printer, 1967, pp. 82-102.

Fenwick, G. Roy, "Some Musical Memories," *Wentworth Bygones*, VI, (1965), pp. 24-30.

Goodale, Edward, "The Origin of Some Street Names of Hamilton," *Wentworth Bygones*, II, (1960), pp. 24-28.

McAuliffe, Gerry, "Crisis," *Hamilton Spectator*, December 26-30, 1967.

Meeker, Josephine, "The Social Geography of Hamilton," B.A. thesis, McMaster University, Hamilton, May, 1953.

Oates, T. W., "From the Little Red School," *The Hamilton Centennial, 1846-1946*, pp. 55-60.

Ontario Association of Architects, Hamilton Chapter, "The Architects Speak Out," *Hamilton Spectator*, August 21-26, 1967.

Reynolds, Ella Julia, "Days Before Yesterday—Music, Art, Drama and Literature," *Hamilton Centennial, 1846-1946*, pp. 47-54.

Spalding, L. T., *The History and Romance of Education (Hamilton), 1816-1950*, Hamilton, 1950.

Thomson, Alexander, "Development of Mountain Due to Vision of T. S. Morris," *Hamilton Herald*, June 28, 1930.

Thomson, Thomas M., *The Spencer Story*, Spencer Creek Conservation Authority, 1965.

Waldon, Freda F., "Early Provision for Libraries in Hamilton," *Wentworth Bygones*, IV, (1963), pp. 22-35.

Waram, J. T. C., "City Planning in Hamilton," *Wentworth Bygones*, IV, (1963), pp. 36-43.

Watson, J. W., "Hamilton and its Environs," *Canadian Geographical Journal*, XXX, (May, 1945), pp. 240-252.

INDEX

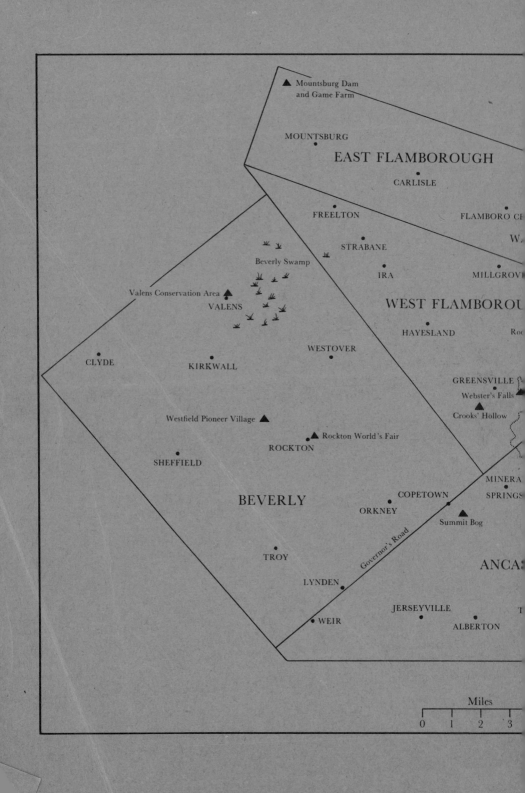

Mountsburg Dam
and Game Farm

MOUNTSBURG

EAST FLAMBOROUGH

CARLISLE

FREELTON

FLAMBORO CI

W.

STRABANE

Beverly Swamp

IRA

MILLGROV

Valens Conservation Area

WEST FLAMBOROU

VALENS

HAYESLAND

Roc

WESTOVER

CLYDE

KIRKWALL

GREENSVILLE

Webster's Falls

Crooks' Hollow

Westfield Pioneer Village

Rockton World's Fair

ROCKTON

SHEFFIELD

MINERA

BEVERLY

COPETOWN

SPRINGS

ORKNEY

Summit Bog

Governor's Road

ANCA:

TROY

LYNDEN

JERSEYVILLE

T

WEIR

ALBERTON

Miles

0 1 2 3